July 4th 2009

Jill i you have
heard the AIR
story many times, bat
i think you will enjoy
some of the inside.

Rescuing the American Dream

The Entrepreneur's Way

By G. Web Ross and Howard A. Klausner

Printed in The U.S.A.
Library of Congress Cataloging-in-Publishing Data is Available on request

ISBN: 978-0-692-00378-7

For Tom Ross, Rob Anthony, and Wayne Gullstad,
Whose lives, character and real-life stories of the
American Dream inspired this book.

CONTENTS

Book Two: The CityForest Story

Prologue

The voice on the other end of the phone was angry, and every other word was one you don't use in mixed company. "Your equipment's busted again! Either fix it or take it out of here!!"

It was after midnight. Tom Ross had just collapsed into an exhausted sleep after an 18-hour day in the 100-square foot office he shared with his business partner and roommate Rob Anthony, who was snoring on the futon in the next room, equally exhausted. No sense in waking him up. It was Tom's turn. The twenty-four year old engineer dressed quickly, and slipped out of the tiny apartment.

It's not a long drive from Portland Oregon to the pulp paper mill in Wauna. But at one o'clock in the morning, with no moon and no other cars on the road, winding through the barren no-mans-land timber and industrial country can seem like a thousand miles—especially when the mind is racing with the most despairing thoughts a young man in his first business can muster.

You see, the first two words of that furious machine operator's tirade said it all: "*Your equipment.*"

It was indeed Tom Ross and Rob Anthony's equipment that was having trouble in the unforgiving 1000-degree+ environment of the main boiler in that pulp paper mill, bringing it to a grinding halt seventy minutes into the swing shift this moonless November night.

And it had happened before.

The 24-year old engineer, who'd made a hard left turn out of another very promising business venture to license the patent on this piece of equipment from a quirky but brilliant inventor, partnered up with his college roommate to start this company <u>with</u> that equipment. He got his Dad and people he loved to invest in this vision that *depended on* that equipment actually *working* and delivering the savings and efficiency he'd looked the owners of this mill in the eye and promised it would. So confident he was, he'd built this business around that piece of equipment that now *wasn't* working?

"Oh, man." Tom closed his eyes as he parked the car in the employee lot. What if it was beyond repair? What if his prototype wrecked the boiler? The guy sounded upset enough to call every single mill in the United States and badmouth the Anthony-Ross Company right into bankruptcy.

What does he say? How does he tell the investors? Will he ever work again? What does he say to his dad? What will Thanksgiving dinner be like for the rest of his life—surely single. I mean, he didn't even have a girlfriend; his life was so wrapped up in this company. Who would marry him now, the biggest failure in the history of American business? The 24-year-old pariah who single-handedly brought this mill in Wauna, Washington to its knees?

Such were the slightly less than rational thoughts of young Tom Ross as the entrepreneur swung the shop door open, took a deep breath, and entered the Wauna mill floor like a dead man walking.

Preface

Why I Wrote This Book

My name is Web Ross, and I am a rich man.

Now, wait. Before you go to work on that thought, I do not own a private jet, a sports team, or a yacht. I'm not a real estate baron, venture capitalist, or rock star CEO on the talk show circuit. I'm not on Bill Gates' or Warren Buffett's Christmas card lists.

I drive my own domestic car, live in a comfortable but "sensible" house, and have never lit a Cuban cigar with a hundred dollar bill. I have enough money to live well, but not really in the lifestyle of the rich and famous. I may not be a talking head business pundit on TV, a politician, or a business school professor, but I have something to say about success and getting rich. And I believe now, more than ever, what I have to say needs to be heard.

So what exactly, then, are my credentials for writing a book about success and, if I don't have all the usual titles and toys, why would I describe myself as a rich man?

I am 80 years old. I was born during the Great Depression, and started my first business when I was eight. I had a successful 30-year run as an executive in the paper business, raised three terrific kids with a wife of sixty years who still speaks to me like we're newlyweds, and I retired with honor.

But that's when this story really begins.

Something has gone terribly wrong in American business. As I write these words in 2009, the landscape of our economy and the very course we are setting as a nation are changing daily into something we've not seen for a long, long time—if ever. Fear, uncertainty, and pessimism hang over this country like a forbidding cloud, and the American Dream suddenly seems like a quaint and irrelevant memory; something from a time long past.

The stock market is worth a little more than half its value from a year ago, erasing trillions in personal wealth. The "experts" tell us it has even farther to fall. The "sub-prime mortgage meltdown" has caused America's oldest and most respected investment banks to disappear - literally. Two of the Big 3 Automakers have thrown in the towel, and thrown *themselves* before the mercy of the federal government, which many of us are now dismayed to see in the car business. CEOs stand hangdog before Congress, hat in hand, looking for their "bailout" as their banking counterparts did to the tune of nearly a trillion dollars last Fall. The same government is writing checks with money it doesn't have for companies and institutions who are "just too big to fail," passing budgets our grandchildren will be yoked and burdened- *and taxed--* with, just to pay down this Himalayan debt we are incurring to nations who, for the first time in history, are beginning to seriously question our credit-worthiness.

Meltdown? Bailouts? Questionable credit?

Just a reminder: for the last hundred years, the United States has led the world economically. The combination of the American can-do, entrepreneurial spirit and our work ethic in a free-market environment has conferred upon us the much-deserved status of "Shining City on the Hill," the most prosperous society the world has ever known.

So what in the world has happened?

There are probably a hundred answers to that question. Most are as complicated and open-ended as the financial "debt instruments" that triggered this catastrophe to begin with. Worse, the national dialogue right now is more focused on fixing blame than fixing the problem, which is about as helpful as putting a band-aid on a tumor. These may be symptoms and factors in this crisis, but they're not answers.

What's happened is simple. We have abandoned the very foundations of the American Dream in our headlong pursuit of wealth, success, comfort, and power. These things are all well and good and have their place, but they are just destinations. They are not what this Journey called life is about. The Journey, the very fuel for this American Dream, is in *what we become in pursuit of these things*. Ultimately, this journey comes down to one thing: our **character**. It is character that made America that shining City on the Hill, and it is our character that will rescue this Dream.

It's time to face some harsh reality. Our economy, our business and corporate cultures, and yes, even our government, have largely turned their backs on the fundamental truths and realities that every small business must live out in the marketplace every single day. These truths are no different for GM, AIG, and Citibank than they are for a one-woman shop on Main Street. They remain just as true in the 21st century as they did in Solomon's day, and they have little to do with "management," "sales and marketing," "networking," or whatever business-speak we could name.

These truths are about character. Follow them, and you will succeed. Ignore them, and you may prosper for a while, but your temple will eventually come crashing down- as we've seen happen to company after company, virtually every day of the past year.

Stimulus packages, industry "czars," and trillion dollar bailouts are not the answer to this crisis. Government intervention may stave off disaster in the short term, but it won't ultimately change anything. Regardless which party holds Congress or the White House, we all know instinctually that political solutions generally make things worse, not better, when it comes to business.

The time has come to take a good long look at ourselves as a nation and as individuals, and recognize an even harder truth: what largely led to this crisis is a character problem. In our warp-speed pursuit of success and riches and all the trappings of the good life, we've watched our corporations, banks, even governmental institutions engage in business practices that would bankrupt any small business and, in many cases, land the practitioner in jail. To a large extent, the rest of us have been left holding the proverbial bag.

But enough on the Problem. I wrote this book to be part of the Solution.

Like so many who've crashed and burned with their excesses and, shall we say, occasional lapses in good judgment, it's time for American Macro-Business to check itself in for a good old-fashioned Rehab. The best way to begin is in looking to the daily reality of American *Micro*-Business. The Answer to this ongoing crisis - indeed, the very key that unlocks the door to a rich and successful business and personal life, the *essence* of the American Dream, is a return to 12 timeless truths, 12 *Steps* if you must, played out in literally millions of small businesses every day in every town in America.

Ultimately, the American Dream isn't about getting rich. The American Dream is all about character.

Now I should tell you that this was not the original message of this book, and I want you to know right up front that this book is not an economic treatise on what's ailing the American economy in 2009 (and hopefully not much further beyond). This is not a jargon-filled textbook, it's not a socio-economic lecture, and it's not a self-important memoir of my illustrious executive career.

The book is just a good story. Two stories, actually, of a still-thriving American Dream, and they happen to be true. I know. I was there.

As to my "illustrious career" as an executive; I had a good run in the pulp paper industry, retiring as President and CEO of Publishers

Paper in 1986. I was part of a major turnaround for a troubled but terrific company that was just beginning to see the fruits of our labors in a complete re-invention of our corporate culture and the way we ran our business. The idea was simple: bottom up-management. Hire (or keep) the best people, let them do their job, and get out of their way while they do it. And man, did it work, beyond even my own always-optimistic expectations. We were poised, not only to revolutionize Publishers Paper, but also to break through to true greatness. Then the volatile pulp paper market and skyrocketing interest rates forced our parent company, Times Mirror, to sell the company. Overnight, it seemed I was out of a job. It was a tough pill to swallow, but it made business sense. They were good to us. They gave their executives a nice send-off with a fine, but not excessive retirement package. In truth, it was the thing a lot of CEOs work and plan toward.

But not for me. Not yet. In my mind, I hadn't finished the job. It was a bittersweet retirement I entered, one that came too soon to a guy too young to hang it up.

But mine is not the story I'm here to tell you.

These are two stories of the American Dream: three young men and two successful start-ups. Average, middle class boys who grew up the way millions of boys and girls do in this country. There was nothing particularly unique or significant in their make-up that separated them from others. Indeed, if anything, there were some challenges in all three that had to be overcome. There was no special giftedness in any of them beyond a drive to succeed, an independent streak, and a basic honesty and goodness.

Yet, two of them together and one separately, these boys grew up, lived and *worked* the American Dream. They started businesses, grew their businesses, and sold those businesses for a terrific profit. By most people's definition, they got rich.

However, it didn't happen quickly, and it wasn't terribly easy getting there. There was a lot of struggle, good luck and bad luck, headaches and heartaches, and just plain *hard work* between open-ing their doors as a new company and signing their "Sold" deal.

Most importantly, what made them rich is not just the well-deserved cash they took with them. It's a lot more than that. They are rich from the people they served, the needs they filled, improve-ments they brought to their industries, and lives that forever were changed because of starting what we might call just an "average" company.

My original title for this book was *Three Entrepreneurs and a Wannabe,* and you can surely guess who's the "wannabe." The fact is, this career executive - and let's be honest, that's still a career *em-ployee* - always wanted to start his own business, but just never got the chance. I always had a job, and I've always enjoyed my work.

In retrospect now, I see my premature retirement as a gift. It made it possible for me to watch these great stories unfold and to play a small part in both of them. Hey, they were start-ups in a busi-ness I knew. I was a career executive with an entrepreneur's heart, and suddenly at age 60, I was available!

One last detail as backdrop: one of the three entrepreneurs is my son, the other two became like sons to me. I got to see the basic life and business lessons my dad taught me, the same truths I tried to teach my son, lived out in both these companies. And you know what? These truths may be as old as history itself, but they still work.

Every time.

For those of you starting a business or *thinking* of starting a business, a student finding your way through school, an executive, a leader, or just a devotee of inspirational, real life success stories, have I got two stories for you. These guys are the poster boys for the American Dream that in spite of the headlines, the omni-present political rancor, and increasingly dire predictions, is alive and well in the Land of the Free.

These stories, these business and life experiences, and these Twelve Steps, truths, fundamentals - call them what you will - all combined to make these maybe-not-so average, hard-working young men rich, in every sense of that word.

They made me rich as well. I'm writing this book because I want you to be rich too.

Web Ross
Little Rock, Arkansas

Why You Should Read This Book

A Note from the Co-Author

I did not want to write this book. Well, let me rephrase that. When Web Ross first told me the stories you're about to read, I was entertained and inspired, but I didn't see what value I could bring to this project. Honestly, I thought it was just too "niche," and its message would only speak to a very limited audience.

Boy was I wrong.

I am a screenwriter by trade. I spend my days telling stories in film and television. I did write an astronaut biography a couple years back, but a life-story is still a story. Not only was I not particularly interested in writing a non-fiction "business book," I did not feel remotely qualified to do so, and feared I might even harm its chances of ever getting published. I mean, what credibility does a movie guy really bring to a book about entrepreneurship?

Then September 2008 happened. Like a lot of people, my perspective on what I do and all things America changed on a dime. When Web called me again at the end of that fateful month, I agreed to head over and listen to these stories one more time. Sitting in his den in Little Rock, Arkansas, the light finally came on for me. This guy not only has two really good American Dream yarns to spin, he's got something important to say to all of us. With sixty years in business, more than twenty as a CEO, his credentials and credibility are more than enough to say it, and remind us before it's too late, of some fundamental truths that this country's government and economy seem to have forgotten.

When he finished, I felt, as the old saying goes, that I wasn't choosing this project, it was choosing *me*.

This book is designed to read exactly as it was told in a series of afternoons in that den, in a few Little Rock eateries and watering holes, and a couple more in Tennessee and Seattle. It's not academic case studies or a lecture. It's two amazing and inspiring stories of real life American Dreams, along with the running commentary and wisdom of a man who not only witnessed those stories, but as an advisor to these men and their Dream (which, as you will see, often entered nightmare territory), he was an integral part of those stories. In its own way, this book is a conversation between the two of us; a seasoned 80-year-old retired CEO and a 40-something writer who suddenly realizes for the first time he's never been anything *but* an entrepreneur. In the end, the Twelve Steps of The Entrepreneur's Way is what Web and I believe to be not only the wisest and surest path to success and true-life riches, but the one true answer to this god-awful economic mess in which this country finds itself in 2009. The way back home is through one simple word: *character*. That's what this book is all about.

As the conversation continued, I kept hearing the same words, the same principles again and again as these guys faced adversity and challenges that most would have completely withered under. Words that don't show up all that much in textbooks, magazines, and business shows, but boy they oughta.

Integrity. Honesty. Transparency. Tenacity. TRUST.

May I ask you a question? In all the drama unfolding before us in Washington and on Wall Street this past year, and in many of the questionable (at best) "solutions" put forth, how much of any of these qualities and traits have you seen? I mean, really seen?

What ultimately drove me to writing this book with Web Ross wasn't so much the stories, or that these young men were so unique or even boy scout in their approach. It's quite the opposite. The light that went on for me was that millions of just regular men and women run their own businesses, and have their own version of these wild and wooly, nail-biting, and ultimately triumphant stories of the American Dream. They are part of this country's character. The American Dream is in our DNA.

No, this isn't a "niche" book. As much as Web and I revere the Way of the Entrepreneur, so much so we used that phrase as our sub-title, we both hold firm that the message of *Rescuing the Dream* is for all of us.

"Character counts" the saying goes. It counts in our selves, our relationships, and, as you will see, it counted mightily in the journey of these three young men and their pursuit of that same American Dream. These Twelve Steps of Character are really Statements of Principle, and were extracted from these stories. They are time-less and practically second nature to anyone who starts and runs any venture or enterprise, whether it's a $50 million, 85-employee pulp paper mill or a one-man screenwriting business. You will see them employed again and again as these guys walk the way of the entrepreneur, which we have found to be synonymous with the best of human character traits in any relational situation, business or otherwise.

However, at the top of our biggest banks, financial institutions, our government, and its management of our economy in the de-cisions and directions that have landed us in the biggest financial crisis since the Great Depression, many (and in some cases *all*) of these truths were cast aside when they became "inconvenient" truths - virtually ignored. You don't need Web or me to tell you that. Read over these Twelve Steps, then open up your newspaper and draw your own conclusion.

This is the reason for the stories, this very book you are about to read. Not only are these Twelve Steps fundamental to the longevity and success of any business, organization, or relationship, they are the only way for a return to what we have come to know and treasure as the American Dream.

No, I didn't want to write this book. *I had to write this book.*

Howie Klausner
Franklin, Tennessee

Introduction

Three Traits, Twelve Steps
The Entrepreneur's Way

Let's get one thing straight. The Way of the Entrepreneur is not for the faint of heart. Starting one's own business is not for someone devoid of passion, someone in need of routine and predictability, and it is certainly not for *anyone* with a low tolerance for risk. The Prologue at the beginning of this book really did happen, and it wasn't the only time Tom Ross and Rob Anthony felt the Business World's Sword of Damocles inching ever closer to their young heads. Wait 'til we get to Wayne Gullstad's story in Book Two.

This is not a chest-thumping declaration of business machismo or whatever is the female equivalent of machismo. This is just truth. As over-the-top as Tom's exhausted and anxious inner dialogue might have been on that dark and stormy night at the beginning of his company's history, it was based in reality. The future of the Anthony-Ross Company really was hanging in the balance.

We'll get to the end of that story in a moment, but please be forewarned. If you start a business, any business in any industry, you will have at least one moment similar to this one, and you will never see it coming. There's not an entrepreneur, anywhere, who doesn't have his or her own version of this same episode.

So maybe you don't have starting a business on your mind. Maybe you're reading this book to see a regular guy's take on character and rescuing the American Dream. Fair enough. This is a book about character and values, but it's also the story of three entrepreneurs who showed extraordinary character and values. Please indulge me for a moment as I ask everyone to ask their self this very simple question. *Am I an Entrepreneur?*

But before you answer, let's get a clear picture of where we are right now. There's an old saying that you won't know where you're going if you don't know where you've been. This is as true for our country as it is for you and me.

A Very Brief Economics History of the Last 80 Years

I promise this is the only textbook-y section of this book. Before we really answer the question of this chapter, we need to understand the broad strokes of this country's business history as the 21st century ramps up to speed. Why? Because the business climate you're in, or about to enter, is not even remotely the same as the one I entered sixty years ago.

The business world is split between two categories of people—employees and owners. As it was in the 1950s when I got my first job out of college, most people are employees, but there the similarities end.

When I entered the adult work force in the middle of the twentieth century, America was in the pedal-to-the-metal industrial boom that put us at the top of the world in pretty much every sense of that term. We'd lived through a Depression, won two World Wars, and were settling down to work. We were laying the interstate highway system, shipping automobiles all over the world, developing jet air travel, inventing plastics and the transistor and television, building cities and homes for the population explosion of the Baby Boom, and launching the most labor-intensive undertaking in human history - landing human beings on the Moon. This country was working 24/7. Jobs were everywhere. It's just what you did when you got out of school or came home from the service. You went to work for somebody.

Now that model isn't gone by any stretch of the imagination. The majority of people still follow that very path. Most working people are employees of a corporation or privately held company. However, the ratio of employees to entrepreneurs has changed dramatically.

Most economists and historians agree that a fundamental shift began as we entered what's known as the Information Age at the end of last century. It isn't that the personal computer, the Internet, and mobile communications replaced the industrial and service economy. They didn't. What they did was to explode the business landscape.

New opportunities, new possibilities, but most importantly new ways of thinking about business are what have ushered in the 21st century. These and a hundred other new technologies have liberated the American workforce, creating huge industries that didn't even exist before 1980, and have exponentially grown the marketplace. And the rate of change accelerates every year.

The biggest change of all? The sense of independence. The free agency, if you will, of the American worker. More people own their own businesses now than at any time in our history. As we watch downsizing, outsourcing, government intervention, and market corrections take their toll on our biggest employers and traditional businesses, that number is accelerating upward as well.

That's all observational and anecdotal. Let's go to the data.

The US Census in 2004 tells the story in numbers. We are right in the middle of a Sea Change. Fully half of the private sector employees in this country work for small businesses (those that employ between 1 and 99 people). 99% of American business firms are small businesses. Hang onto your hats for this one, folks. More than ¾ of all U.S. businesses have no payroll employees. That translates to 20 million people running their own enterprise, solo.

The reality of this Sea Change and the point of this book lie within this data. We are no longer a nation of employees. We are a nation of Entrepreneurs.

That's enough history. Let's get back to my Question.

What is it that makes one an entrepreneur? Well, really, there's no such thing as a profile business owner. Of those millions of people the Census identified, we find Blacks, Whites, Asians, Latinos, Native Americans, and every other race, creed, and color group you can think of. It's still more men than women starting their own businesses, but that number is evening out rapidly. Age seems to be no factor. They can be as young as teenagers, or older than me. Indeed, the AARP reports that as baby boomers retire (and their 401Ks slide downhill, sad to say), more senior citizens than ever will be starting their own businesses in the years ahead.

Is there a common thread? Is there a trait or a pattern shared by all who hang out a shingle, quit their 9-5 jobs, graduate from business school, or come out of retirement with the sole objective of starting their own business?

Yes, there is. Three things are common to all entrepreneurs everywhere: passion, an independent spirit, and the willingness to take on risk. They exist in varying degrees, but all three must be present if the owner of a business has any hope of truly succeeding.

I. Passion – Your Business and Your People, You Gotta Care

There is an old saying. *Nobody cares what you know 'til they know how much you care.*

Let's get back to Tom, and put an average employee in the Prologue scene. Let's call him a project engineer, taking that call after midnight. Does that engineer on the payroll of a company roll himself out of bed after an 18-hour workday, and head up that dark winding highway to a pulp paper mill in the middle of nowhere or, for heaven's sake, just wait 'til morning? Truth is, it could probably wait 'til then.

Now don't get me wrong. A lot of employees, including the ones who would eventually work for Tom and Rob, would certainly drive up that highway, just because they do care. However, Tom and Rob had looked the owners and managers of this mill in the eye and given their word. This piece of equipment would work, and it would dramatically improve their operation. These people were counting on that promise, and they'd paid for the installation of a prototype. If it worked, they'd order the whole system and the Anthony Ross Company was off to the races, but if it didn't…

You see, it wasn't just a paycheck or an account on the line here, the future of Tom's company depended on this machine working as advertised. That 18-hour day he'd just spent in the office had been spent like just about every other day - at the drafting table, on the phone, and poring over test data - all devoted to making that machine better, more efficient, more reliable, and less expensive to manufacture. A machine most people have never heard of, in a process even fewer understand.

That process serves virtually every person in the world, every day of their lives. Think I'm exaggerating? Imagine your day without paper. Reading, writing, personal hygiene are just the beginning.

And Tom and Rob had been laboring with this piece of equipment every working day - all day and most weekends - for eighteen months. A year and a half, and they'd not received a dime. Only the stockholders' initial investment made it possible for the partners to actually move out of the basement of my house and into that cracker box apartment so that they could rent an office. An office that was so small each had to take turns stepping out into the hall when their one phone line would ring so one could concentrate on the call and not feel self-conscious with the other, two feet away on the other side of the same desk.

Oh yeah, they paid themselves the princely executive sum of $4500 a year.

Tom Ross wasn't an employee; he was a founding partner. His name was on the door alongside Rob Anthony's name. There was a lot more at stake here than just some money. There was his reputation, the future of his business, and even his future life. And now, add in the frustration of something this owner-engineer had put nearly two years of his life into, not working properly.

That guy rolls out of bed and heads for his car in the middle of the night because this isn't just his job, this is his passion. This is his business.

That's the heart of character.

II. The Spirit of Independence – The Dominant Trait

If the working world can be defined by two basic roles, employee and owner, it can also be sub-divided into two psychological categories: those who can comfortably work for others and those who just can't.

You'll notice I use the word *comfortably*. This also is very general and observational, so let's go back to the data and see what we find when we drill down a bit. A recent Gallup poll revealed that 85% - *that's 85 percent!* - of Americans either don't like their job or don't care for the style, personality, or leadership of their employer/ supervisor.

This tells us one of two things: 1) 85% of our work force is working for idiots or, 2) a sizable portion of that 85% would rather be working for no one at all.

Now let's go ahead and dismiss one side of this curve, those who simply don't need to work in the first place, and dismiss the other extreme, those people who just don't get along with others very well. This still leaves a sizable amount of people dissatisfied with their employment.

There's one last piece of data for this subject of independence. The average American's working career will involve seven major job changes. Seven. Though surely many of these people are recruited away, or the choice isn't theirs when they change or lose a job, or maybe they spot wonderfully logical advances in their pre-planned career trajectory and, God bless 'em, common sense and observation tell us what we know instinctually. We're all looking for something more, and it's not necessarily more money. There is something deeper and more powerful running through the human spirit, and an average of seven changes of career tells us we're not finding it at that next place. Still, we never stop looking.

The spirit of independence is not quite as clear-cut as passion. By no means does it imply that only owners are leadership oriented and employees aren't. I was a CEO, my very job description was Leading, but I was still an employee. Most of the employees I had the privilege of working with were very independent minded and leaders themselves. Yet we were on a team. We believed in our company and our business, and most of us were lucky enough to like what we did, but we all answered to someone whose decision power superseded our own.

The simple truth is that if you're working for someone else, your time, at least those 40+ hours a week you're on the job, does not ultimately belong to you. That's the trade-off for a regular paycheck, benefits, and having a place that allows you to do whatever it is you have chosen to do with your professional life. Whether from necessity or choice, that's good enough for the majority of people working for someone, even those 85% who choose to stay in whatever job, despite their dissatisfaction.

For those individuals who are inspired by an idea or a plan for a business, or those who just don't want their decisions or their destiny in the hands of someone else, it isn't good enough.

Which leads us to the final thread common to all entrepreneurs...

III. Risk – The Willingness to Take the Plunge

The Oxford Dictionary defines the word Entrepreneur as "...one who starts a business and incurs the financial risk."

Now we can talk about passion and an independent spirit all day long, but here is where the proverbial rubber meets the proverbial road. An entrepreneur, by the dictionary's definition, is a risk taker. One might even say the ULTIMATE risk-taker. More than any of these three basic factors, this is the one that will -it *must* - drive your answer to The Question of this opening chapter. *Am I an Entrepreneur?*

First off, I might take issue with the good folks at Oxford. As you're going to see in the story of Tom and Rob with the Anthony Ross Company, and again in Wayne Gullstad with a company called CityForest, starting your own business does indeed entail risk, but it's a lot more than money. There is the risk of TIME. Yes, this is the perspective of an eighty-year old man who counts every day as precious, but we all know this truth to be self–evident. Our time is worth vastly more than money. There is always more money to be made out there somewhere, and lost money can be made up eventually. That is not so with time. When time has been spent, it's gone forever.

Hear this one loud and clear as you ponder your answer to The Question. No matter how much money and time you invest, no matter how great or necessary your product or service, or how bulletproof your plan, these are no guarantees of success. It is true. The greater the risk, the greater the reward. But don't ignore the other side of that equation. The greater the risk, the greater the loss if it doesn't work out...and it might not.

Tom Ross and Rob Anthony had put eighteen months of working six and seven long days every week for essentially no pay into that piece of equipment we've been discussing. Their company was operating on the financial investment of people they cared deeply for, and felt personally responsible for every nickel of that investment. They lived their professional and personal lives centered on the 12 Step Principles of Success this book is about.

But if that piece of equipment fails that night, it's Game Over. That eighteen months and the investment capital they'd raised is gone forever. Second chance? Not likely. The industry they chose is a tight-knit community who talk among themselves. Word of the failure of their prototype would be industry-wide in no time. Tom's inner dialogue may have been a bit dramatic and leaning heavily on the worst-case-scenario, but it was coming from an engineer's objective and sober calculation:

I can fail here.

In 1984, I was the CEO of Publishers Paper, owned by the Times Mirror organization. After thirty years in the paper business, I knew it pretty well, and I'd done fairly well in it. So when we received word that Times Mirror would be selling our company, I looked long and hard at my options.

I'd always wanted to have my own business, and suddenly here was one right in my grasp. I understood it, I knew the people, I knew the market, and I knew this company's strengths and weaknesses intimately after running it for seven years.

They would sell it to me. I could raise the necessary capital, but I would have to pledge every single thing I owned. I was president when we turned this company around. I knew I could not only make it work, I could make it more profitable than ever.

But… *every single thing I owned*? I had three young adult kids, one an entrepreneur, one finishing medical school, and another just starting college.

I had to let it go. I couldn't afford the risk.

And Now - Back to Tom Ross and that Dark and Fateful Night

You must forgive the drama. I loved radio cliffhangers as a kid.

So what happened out at the Wauna Paper Mill? When we last saw Tom, he was entering the now-quiet mill. Unnaturally quiet. All eyes locked on him as he walked across the floor to the main boiler. Not a smile to be found. The millwrights, the foreman, even the operators -"these guys were mad."

In probably the greatest dramatic performance of his life, the 24-year old strides across the floor with a look of quiet confidence, nodding politely at the stone cold faces. He's trying to look like he'd done this successfully a hundred times before, while his insides are roiling more furiously than that main boiler when it's going at capacity.

Quick reminder: To quote the movie Apollo 13, "failure is not an option." If he doesn't get this thing working—and fast—this will probably spell the end of the Anthony-Ross Company.

He checks the first window. Cracked. Dirty. He circles around the massive barrel to the firebox, and sees the carnage. It doesn't look good. Mounting bracket shaken loose from the vibration. (*Gotta make that bracket stronger.*)

He pulls the cleaning rod from the boiler. Still intact, just gunked up with the black "liquor" residue from the heating process. Calmly ignoring the entire third shift watching his every move, he cleans the rod down, changes the cleaning tip, reassembles the unit itself, jury rigs a new mount, and applies power.

Works perfectly.

He nods to the foreman, "Okay. You're good to go."

And as the operator gives him a thumbs-up, the entrepreneur, the founding partner of the Anthony-Ross Company strides right back out into the Oregon night, already in his head, redesigning that bracket he'd be working on by 8 the next morning.

◆ ◆ ◆

So let's return to The Question. *Are you an Entrepreneur?* Have the three foundational traits of all successful business owners - passion, independence, and the willingness to take a risk - made the answer obvious? Some will surely answer yes, many will say no. But before you write the answer in the margin, or resign yourself to a destiny you're still not sure of, let me break my earlier promise and offer you one final hint from the pages of history.

On a sweltering hot day in Philadelphia more than 200 years ago, a group of men fixed their signature to a document every schoolchild in the United States still studies today. If you are an American, you probably know at least part of it by heart. You certainly recognize the names signed with a quill pen at the bottom of it. However, this open letter to the King of England and these men's compatriots is more than just an historic relic found under glass in our nation's capital.

It is a Declaration of a mightily independent spirit. It positively shouts to the world and all of history the fiery passion of Thomas Jefferson, John Adams, James Madison, Ben Franklin, John Hancock, and all the others gathered there, as well as those who sent them there. Passion not only for their independence, but to make theirs and their children's world better.

And *risk?* The Declaration of Independence was effectively a declaration of war. Even with their own version of 12 steps for success, the risk to these men was very real. They might not succeed. When they signed a pledge of their "lives, fortunes, and sacred honor," there was every possibility they would lose all three. In defying the mightiest nation on Earth in 1776, odds were that each of them would forfeit their treasure, their homes, their livelihoods, and their freedom - at the very least. Truth told, should Britain prevail, they all would surely hang for treason, and an independent United States would remain just a dream.

This nation was founded on passion, independence, and the willingness to take the ultimate risk. Whether you're working 9 to 5 for a company, planning to launch the next great start-up, soon to graduate with an idea better than Google, a newly laid off employee with an idea, or someone just trying to make his or her own business, personal enterprise, or even family that much better, know this:

You are indeed living in a nation of Entrepreneurs. The Twelve Steps to Success in your professional and personal life are in the lifeblood and foundational character of this country. We can talk bailout and stimulus packages all day long, and print money 'til we're out of ink, but the only way to right the ship of our Economy and re-assume our rightful place as The Shining City on the Hill, is to return to these same principles that some may have forgotten.

So listen up. Turn the page. I'm going to tell you two stories of the American Dream, the stories of three men who were off the charts in their passion, independence, and willingness to take a risk. As you read the trials, tribulations, and ultimately the *triumphs* of The Anthony-Ross Company and CityForest, two average, but great American companies with extra-ordinary histories, I urge you to watch these stories unfold with the Twelve Steps - these foundational principles of success in action. Watch as these men practice each of these Twelve Steps, in their business, in their respect and treatment of their customers, and in their lives.

You will see for yourself how they turned out.

The Twelve Steps of Success

1. I Care.

2. I Don't Quit.

3. "It's Gonna Work."

4. I Tell the Truth.

5. I Keep My Word.

6. I Refuse to Quit.

7. I Never Stop Learning.

8. I Will Be Lucky and I Will Be Unlucky Too.

9. I Sweat the Small Stuff.

10. I Make Decisions.

11. I Am Worthy of Trust.

12. I Accept the Risk.

Book One

The Anthony-Ross Story

Chapter One
Rob Anthony and Tom Ross
The Journey to a Start-up

"I'm gonna be a millionaire when I'm 30, Dad."

I'm not sure I took it seriously when my junior-high aged son told me this, breezing in after school one day. Predictably, at 13 he didn't exactly have a clear idea *how* he would reach this lofty perch, but what most sticks in my memory is that there was no childish bravado in the statement. It was a calm, nearly indifferent belief and plan for his life. As children tend to be, he was completely secure in the knowledge that whatever his mind could conceive, he could indeed achieve.

Tom Ross was born in February of 1959 in Everett, Washington. He was three when we moved to Crossett, Arkansas, and there he would spend the majority of his childhood. I'd like to tell you he had the mark of something "special". The truth is that there was no mark of Donald Trump or Jack Welch or Bill Gates there, no hint of greatness or "chosen" status. He was just a good, solid kid, like a zillion other good, solid kids.

Money was never a big focus in our house. I don't remember giving Tom or my other two children allowances. They were just paid for the bigger chores, like mowing the lawn or raking the leaves. The declared future millionaire really wasn't fixated on being "rich." Matter of fact, as the son of a company president and a boy who spent his afternoons and summers as a glorified laborer and making friends among those laborers, Tom was actually a tad uncomfortable with the fact that we were fairly successful. Not really the picture of the driven young mogul, except for the fact that he didn't just "not mind working," he really enjoyed it.

Tom's first job was selling newspapers in downtown Crossett for ten cents apiece. He was a camp counselor and a bunch of other part-time jobs, but his favorite was grease-monkey'ing at the local lumberyard and the sawmill I ran. It wasn't just oiling and lubing the heavy machinery for four bucks an hour, he actually got to *drive* that heavy machinery around the yards in between oil changes. That wasn't a job to him; it was paid recess.

Tellingly, Tom was not only fascinated by the "family business," he gravitated naturally toward it. I got him a job at the absolute entry level of a pulp paper mill, and he was instantly at home. The machinery, the heat, the noise, the smell—he loved it all. He was the stereotypical boy, coming home grimy, sweaty, and grinning every day in the summer and weekends during school.

But there was one special quality about the boy that does bear mentioning. Tom was born with dyslexia.

We in the twenty-first century have grown accustomed to this term, along with several other common learning "disorders." We now know that different cognitive processes are as common to the human condition as different eye color, and are no indicator at all of intelligence. In 1970, that was not really the case. We understood far less then about how the mind processes information. By and large, kids that had trouble reading, spelling, or even concentrating were generally grouped together as "Special-Ed" or worse, *slow*. In many cases, they were segregated from the other kids to undertake an excruciatingly repetitive, remedial approach to "learning." "I have this awful memory," Tom laughs gently, shaking his head, "of this *special class* using these really fat pencils. I don't know if they helped or not, maybe they did, but I was very, very aware that the other kids were using the *skinny pencils*."

Now I know what you're thinking as you read this. What do fat pencils and Tom's dyslexia have to do with the Entrepreneur's Way and 12 Steps to Success?

Everything.

Whether it was clear to Tom that a remedial "special" education would keep him from his stated goal of a million in the bank by thirty, or just the plain embarrassment of being separated from his friends at school, it just would not do. Under my wife Ella Lee's careful direction, we sought out educators with different approaches to learning. Tom attacked this "problem" the same way he later would as an engineer and an entrepreneur: with patience, focus, and a dogged determination *every single day* to solve it. He and his mother worked long hours together, reinventing the way he learned.

This is by no means an educational methods study, and his method would probably work only for him, but here's the point. Tom recognized he needed to look at this challenge from a different perspective than just working harder and doing more repetitions of the same things that weren't working before with fat pencils. He would have to approach reading and writing differently than other people, and work a helluva lot harder.

And he did. I'd like to tell you it was an overnight success. It wasn't. It never got easy. By the time he was a senior in high school, he was one of the "achievers," making A's and applying to engineering schools. He was accepted to Oregon State for the fall of 1977.

On the other side of the country, another American boy was making A's and B's *without* working that hard at it. It is true that for some, learning and school aren't a matter of dogged determination; it just comes easier to them. However, that doesn't mean the rest of life comes any easier. There's always something.

Rob Anthony was born in Klamath Falls, Oregon in August of 1959. He came from farm stock. His father grew up working the family farm in his youth before enlisting to fight in the Korean War.

He was an entrepreneur himself, running several successful businesses while raising his family. Rob's mother was a devout Christian, who not only taught him the value of prayer and a spiritual life, but a love for the faith that would stamp the personal and professional journey of his life.

Bright, freckle-faced, well-mannered All-American church-going boy with a bright future. Right? Sure. But like all of us, the outer picture can often mask an inner struggle, and Rob had one or two.

As a boy, Rob struggled with a stammer.

It could be that his thoughts were simply developing much faster than his ability to speak them, or he had a genuine speech impediment. More than one of his childhood friends remembers that he had a difficult time expressing himself. This would frustrate anybody, and perhaps explains a key part of his personality. Rob Anthony was a fiery *competitor*.

His growing up years weren't so much focused on learning methods or school at all, really. Most of his energies were put toward three things: football, basketball, and baseball. Not particularly gifted with enormous size, he-man strength, or blazing speed, however, Rob was smart enough to figure out a way to excel at all three sports throughout high school. How? By passion, understanding the game he was playing, and finding a way to win.

"I really hated to lose," he remembers now. "I guess that's all well and good until that gets you thrown out of a few games."

Thrown out of few games?

"Oh yeah, I got tossed out of a baseball game for slinging my helmet after a called third strike (*I still say that pitch was high*). And after my fourth foul in a basketball game, I was suddenly able to express myself very well to the ref. He nailed me with a technical, which was number five, which fouled me out. Those are the first two that come to mind," he smiles sheepishly.

It is doubly ironic today to hear an ordained minister of the gospel acknowledge his early struggles with a stammer and an explosive temper on the athletic field, but we're getting ahead of the story.

Rob graduated easily and started college at a small Baptist school before transferring to Oregon State to study engineering.

"Can you understand a word this guy is saying?" The freckle-faced All American sophomore anxiously whispered to the lanky guy next to him, whose brow was furrowed in frustration.

"Not since the first class," was Tom Ross' answer back to Rob Anthony. "Is he from India?"

"I thought it was Pakistan."

Not that it made any difference. True enough, American universities were inundated in the late 70s with brilliant mathematicians and scientists from Asia and the Middle East, and this particular PhD was one of the finest. But a brilliant lecture is pretty much a waste of breath when the lecturer can't be understood. The chalkboard was filled with Einsteinian formulas and equations, but with this professor's thick accent, he might as well have been speaking in his native tongue.

They'd been in this calculus class for three weeks, had even passed in the hall of their student apartment building, but this was the first time Tom and Rob had actually spoken to one another.

"Man, I am just… lost," Rob sighed.

Tom nodded. "Me too. Good thing it's only just the midterm Friday, huh?"

They met at the library that night, figured out enough of the lecture notes to get through the midterm, and they studied together for the rest of their years at OSU.

As a course of study, engineering is not for the undisciplined or the occasionally serious student. It is just about the most challenging field one can choose, filled with mathematics and advanced science. But… survive it, and do well, you'll never be without a job.

If indeed, it's a "job" you're looking for.

At the end of their senior year, Tom and Rob were required to present an industrial design to the faculty. Their study-group had become a close friendship, and Tom had talked Rob into switching from civil to mechanical engineering. It was perfectly logical for the two of them to partner up for this Senior Project together. They executed a solid piece of engineering, a ground-breaking design and prototype for a Flow-Meter with a nuclear power application.

They got an A and, more significantly, a strong recommendation by their professor to take their Flow Meter to Bingham-Willamette, the company that had sponsored their research. At the very least, there would surely be plum job offers to follow.

Which takes us back to that "job" thing.

The world always needs engineers. Small companies, large companies, governments, even the military - all offer great job packages loaded with perks for grads of good engineering schools. It's a great, smart job choice…

Unless that grad's looking for something more than a "job."

The Anthony-Ross Flow-Meter was indeed groundbreaking. They knew it. The data it collected was crucial to the nuclear power industry. Remember, this was the late 70s when that business was still growing. Their method was repeatable. All they really needed to do was get the electronics in a box, "and we're off to the races."

"Rob, we can sell this thing to every pump manufacturer in the industry."

"Yeah, Tom, but we're… engineers. Do we know how to run a business?"

Tom was one step ahead of him on that one, and had signed up classes starting a week later at OSU to complete a minor in Business. The plan was simple: after graduation, they'd improve the design, file the patent together, absolutely wow their sponsoring company with a demonstration, and launch their company once Tom had written a business plan.

Here marks the genesis of Anthony-Ross and Associates, two brash and confident 21-year old high tech-entrepreneurs and their Business School pizza and beer buddies as consultants, out to corner the world market on nuclear pump Flow-Meters.

Off to the Races, indeed.

Chapter Two
Running a Different Race

He was an odd guy. There's just no other way to put it. Thick, horn-rimmed glasses, mostly bald head, hard hat sliding down over his eyes as he pedaled a rusty old bike across the vast Longview, Washington Weyerhaeuser Pulp and Paper Mill grounds, humming a Mormon hymn, lost in his thoughts. Known to tell jokes that were gut-busters to him, and him alone.

If you were casting the part of the geeky, nutty professor inventor guy stuck in the early 60s, Byron Goodspeed would be your man, even wearing a pocket protector. He nearly turned his bike over crossing the Mill Yard when a hopelessly lost Rob Anthony called out to him, interrupting his reverie.

"Excuse me sir, can you help me?"

"I don't know. What do you need help with?"

"It's my first day here. I'm looking for the Recovery Boiler."

"Oh, now that's interesting, very interesting indeed."

Pause.

Rob was getting the distinct idea he was getting the rookie treatment. "Okay, why is that interesting?"

"I just happen to be the chief millwright on the Recovery Boiler, and that's where I'm going."

"Lucky for me," Rob whispered to himself, forcing an enthusiastic smile.

The Big Pitch Meeting for the Flow Meter the summer before was a disaster. Rob had set up a small demonstration through Todd Hill, who had interned with Rob, and was now working for Bingham Willamette. He'd briefed a couple friendly execs who were familiar with what they were doing. This was a great opportunity to possibly get the company to finance the continued development and roll-out of the Flow Meter, become their strategic partner, and get Anthony-Ross and Associates up and operating. With a bit of nervous energy, still, the boys were brimming with confidence as they were escorted by Todd into the conference room...

Which was filled, standing room only (and not much of that) with the entire executive team of Bingham Willamette Industries. So much for the "small demonstration." Two friendly faces, the rest utterly blank. Maybe even a tad hostile.

Hostile? That may be too strong a word, but the memo had said these two engineering students were here to sell them a ground-breaking Flow Meter that, in their view, they'd already paid for. Remember, Bingham Willamette had sponsored the research for their Senior Project at OSU.

Undaunted (well, reasonably undaunted) after the initial pleasantries, Rob launched into his confident, well-rehearsed presentation of how this flow meter would change the face of pump-water monitoring in the nuclear industry and countless other industries that utilized water as a cooling or lubricating agent. Tom quickly set up the demonstration, waiting for the "Go" call. When he got the Big Nod from Rob, he applied power and...

It didn't work.

Tom furiously dove in, head first, disassembling and reassembling, plugging and unplugging as Rob continued on, vamping. Rob doesn't remember if his youthful stammer came back, but I know mine would've.

Friend that he was, Todd jumped in, too, with some impressive projections and marketplace statistics, *anything to distract them!* -

while Tom sweated and prayed desperately under his breath as he manically tore down and rebuilt their Flow Meter. He finally got power to the thing, but it didn't really work. Just kinda sat there and blinked.

The management team excused themselves, none too pleased at losing an hour of a work day. Bingham Willamette would clearly not be strategically partnering with Anthony Ross and Associates in the foreseeable future.

I had moved back to Portland. Rob had been living with us for that summer. He and Tom continued working on the Flow Meter, but it was pretty obvious that the stars were not lining up on this one. There were a lot of complications in the design. So many bugs yet to work out, they really had no practical experience in the nuclear industry, an industry whose bottom was falling out in the aftermath of Three Mile Island.

It was tough to watch Tom and Rob take one on the chin, but that's business. Truth is, most start-ups don't make it. But they were young, smart, and not about to quit. It was a good invention, just not fully developed and the timing wasn't quite right. This wasn't a death blow, just a "learning experience" in the school of hard knocks.

Tom threw himself back into his business classes, and Rob moved up to Washington State to take a full-time engineering job with Weyerhaeuser. They continued meeting every other weekend. They would never completely give up on this thing, but I could see time and distance begin to take their toll. Still, their dream never faltered. They'd gotten their first taste of running their own business, and yeah, like many of us on our first time out, got their butts kicked, but the Entrepreneur Hook was set.

They'd be back.

Rob was having a tough time keeping up with Millwright Byron Goodspeed, both figuratively and literally, as they made their way to the Recovery Boiler. The guy talked a mile a minute, and pedaled merrily along as though Rob was on a bike too (he wasn't).

"You're an engineer, then, Mr. Anthony?"

"Yes sir, I am."

"You one of those R&D fellows?"

"Yes sir."

"You don't have to call me sir. My name's Byron."

"Nice to meet you, Byron. I'm Rob."

"So what do they want you to R&D on the boiler?"

"We're developing a laser to better measure the temperature."

"Excellent idea, Rob. Laser's about the only thing that can handle that heat. Here we are, by the way."

Now I realize most of you know or care very little about the intricacies of pulp paper production, but a little non-technical background is important here. A boiler is exactly what it sounds like, an enormous industrial cooker, generating a spectacular amount of heat. It is fundamental to the production of wood pulp and paper. No matter how much this process has advanced technically, it still comes down to generating a lot of heat to make it work.

You probably remember from sixth grade science class that to make fire, you need two things: fuel and air. So these gargantuan boilers have air vents, or ports, all around their perimeter to keep a steady airflow. These ports have the habit of clogging regularly, as they are filled with the gunky residue of the heating process, what we call "black liquor." Since time immemorial, the only way to keep those ports unclogged and the boiler doing its job was to have a man walking that perimeter, jamming a long rod through each port to keep it clear. It was hot, tedious, and very dangerous work.

Byron Goodspeed's job as millwright was to maintain the recovery boiler and keep it in working order. It didn't take a rocket scientist to see this rod-jamming technique was not exactly the model of modern industrial efficiency. It's just the way they'd always done it.

However, Byron was a problem solver and, at his core, an inventor. He'd been tinkering in the shop with a device he'd fabricated to actually do this job *automatically*.

One last detail here, and it's an important one. As the slightly awkward, bad-joke telling Mormon millwright who pedaled around the yard lost in his own world most times, Byron wasn't exactly viewed as one of Weyerhaeuser's Think Tank. Sadly, he had been the butt of a few jokes over the years here at Longview. He was sensitive to this perception, and had learned to just do his job and keep mostly to himself.

But Rob Anthony wasn't like other people. He liked Byron and recognized a razor-sharp mind. The two of them formed an instant friendship, and before the day was out, Byron was demonstrating the first working model of his prize invention, an automatic port cleaner.

"It was kind of a contraption, to be honest," Rob remembers now. "Jury-rigged, put together with whatever spare parts he had lying around, but you could see the thinking behind it was just genius."

"Have you shown this to the company?" Rob asked the proud inventor.

Byron's face fell. "Uh… yes. I did." He shrugged nonchalantly, but Rob got the feeling that the management either just didn't get it, or worse, they were humoring Byron, viewing him as a loyal hourly employee with a little busy-work project instead of the potential solver of a problem they didn't even know they had.

When he got back to his yet-to-be furnished apartment that night, Rob called his partner in the semi-dormant Anthony-Ross and Associates. "Tom, can you come up to Longview? There's something you need to see."

Tom got it. He didn't need any background or technical briefing. He'd practically grown up in a paper mill. He knew what a recovery boiler was, and instantly saw the same thing Rob did.

It turns out that over time, and maybe this was simply from Rob's obvious interest in Byron's invention, the guys at Weyerhaeuser took notice eventually. With much fanfare, they summoned Byron to the front office to make him an offer to license his invention. In the time-honored spirit of corporate far-sightedness and partnership with their people... the offer was embarrassingly low.

Byron was well into his fifties. A loyal company man, he'd given the best years of his life to this job. He lived, breathed, and thought about little else, other than his family, his God, and the production of pulp paper. It was the passion of this gentle, deeply caring man's professional life. And at best, Weyco was throwing him a bone.

But where Byron was devastated, Tom and Rob saw a once in a lifetime opportunity.

Chapter Three
So Long Flow Meter, Hello APC

Tom watched for the Washington State Patrol as he bombed back down Interstate 5 to Portland, just long enough to pack up his papers and a change of clothes. He was back in Rob's Longview apartment that night, writing a new business plan.

Tom and Rob were on the clock, and they knew it. Weyerhaeuser would figure it out eventually. This wasn't just a gizmo crafted by a bored millwright in his downtime to keep their boiler nice and clean and airy. It would take some serious design work, a lot of testing, and surely a fair amount of money. But an Automatic Port Cleaner would substantially increase the efficiency of the boiler, and therefore the process at the heart of pulp paper production during a national energy crisis!

Let me be more specific with an analogy from our own everyday world. Fuel, I'm sure I don't need to tell you, costs money. Your car, for example. If you could make your 20 miles-per-gallon vehicle perform at 40 mpg, you are now buying half the gas to go the same distance. That would save most people a lot of dough. Same principle here. The ability to keep the boiler's air vents, the ports, constantly clear of obstruction would keep that boiler running at maximum heat and efficiency, using the least amount of fuel, saving that mill real money.

Weyerhaeuser of course knew all about efficiency. They and everybody else in the business knew a clean boiler meant less fuel consumed. Common sense, but there was no real way to measure the results. Remember the timeframe. The industrial use of the computer was still in its infancy in the 80s. Besides, having a guy jamming the rod through the ports every hour seemed to work fine because (all together now)...

It's the way they'd always done it.

Let me cut right to the chase. Tom and Rob knew what they were looking at. They were engineers educated at a great school. Ironically, each had taken an elective class in boiler design, so they understood this process immediately. What they saw was a machine that would work 24/7 without needing a break or food or anything, automating this dangerous process with a precision and constancy a man with a steel rod could never hope to achieve.

And when I say "saving that mill money," I mean hundreds of thousands of dollars per year per mill. Money in the bank. Here, as the computer folks would put it, is the Killer App.

Tom and Rob, from their School of Hard Knocks experience with the Flow Meter, knew how to measure these energy savings. *They could prove it.*

The silence was deafening. Tom and Rob held their breath as Nancy Goodspeed, the millwright's wife finished reading the last page of their proposal, and calmly laid it on the table. She furrowed her brow, deep in thought.

It had been a nice dinner, filled with friendly chit-chat and a few of Byron's jokes that sailed right over Tom and Rob's head. They laughed anyway. Rob and Byron had grown very close the last couple of weeks, their religion being a common bond. An evangelical Christian and a Mormon surely have profound philosophical differences, but their respect for one another was obvious, as was their faith in a loving Creator.

But this gathering was about business.

Byron was married to a sharp woman. Nancy had a keen financial and marketing mind, and was as much his business partner as his wife. He very wisely never made a significant decision without her.

"So, let me be clear," Nancy finally spoke. "You want to market my husband's invention?"

"That's right, Nancy." Tom nodded.

"We have an offer already. You know that."

"Do you think it's a fair offer?" Tom responded gently.

No answer.

"Rob and I don't think it's fair at all, and I don't think you do, either."

"Neither does our attorney." She smiled now, giving them a tiny opening before zeroing in. "If I may be direct, I didn't see any mention of a license fee here."

"It would be a nominal sum," Tom answered, "with a substantially higher royalty."

"Your company is not financed?"

"We're working on that, but… no ma'am. Not yet."

"Rob, what experience do you and Tom have marketing an industrial product?"

"Not as much as we'd like, but—"

"And how old are you gentlemen again?"

"Twenty-two."

"We're toast." Tom shook his head as he pulled out of the Goodspeeds' driveway.

"You think? I thought she was just playing Bad-Cop. Byron likes our plan."

"Twenty-two," Rob. "That was the coffin nail. She's not taking us seriously because she thinks we're kids."

Rob nodded slowly. "They've **got** kids. He's still an hourly guy. He's really counting on this, and he's awfully loyal to this company."

"They're taking advantage of him," Tom added, driving on, clearly disappointed.

"It's a lot to ask, when you think about it," Rob sighed. "Leaving money on the table and going with us. Couple guys right out of college with a business plan and no money. I guess you're right. Their offer may be an insult, but it is something."

They drove on in silence, neither saying a word as they rolled to a stop at a light. Tom groaned out loud suddenly, "Oh man."

"What?"

"I left my jacket."

Tom and Rob were halfway out the door the second time that night, jacket in hand when Nancy stopped them. "You know… it's not a bad plan." They stopped indeed, and turned. She was softer now, obviously not playing Bad Cop anymore. "This is a big decision, fellows. I'm not making any promises, but we will think about this. Can you give us a few days to give you an answer?"

"Uh… yeah."

Monday morning, Byron pedaled up to the Recovery Boiler with a thoughtful look on his face. Rob was deep in some laser-oriented task, didn't even notice him for a moment.

"Do you think God speaks to us in dreams?" Byron asked.

"I guess." Rob kept working, didn't even turn around. "I just hope He doesn't talk to me that way. I can't remember my dreams."

"I had a doozy last night," Byron continued, zipping up his coveralls and getting out his tools. "I was flying, right over this mill, and I could see my port cleaners working on the boiler."

"I don't know if that's God talking, Byron. I think you're just seeing into the future. It's a great invention you've got."

"My wife and my lawyer think you guys are too young and inexperienced."

"We figured that."

"My kids are going to be college age soon enough. We're barely making it as it is. I don't have any idea how I'm gonna pay for that.

I thought maybe if I could sell this invention to the company, I wouldn't get rich, but heck, it would sure help. And then…I met you guys. I haven't been sleeping, Rob."

Rob put down the laser box. "Byron, you have to think of your family first. Tom and I totally understand that. There's no hard feelings, man. None."

"So we talked 'til two last night," Byron continued, like he hadn't even heard him. "I fell asleep finally and had that dream. Woke up this morning like I'd slept for a week. I haven't felt this good in ten years.

"I like you and I trust you. My wife feels the same." He broke into a broad grin. "We're going with Anthony-Ross, Rob. What do you say we get started?"

It wasn't just that they were nice guys who treated Byron with respect. Nancy could see as clearly as her husband that Tom and Rob were sharp, ambitious engineers, even if they were still wet behind the ears. It was beyond clear that they were going to succeed as a partnership, whether it was with Byron's Automatic Port Cleaner or another product.

They also knew that Byron's invention would require a lot of engineering modification before it was ready to market. Although the only money Tom and Rob could offer was the patent fee, which would remain under Byron's name, Byron would receive 8% of every unit sold.

Tom and Rob had studied the market closely. They estimated a selling range of $300,000-500,000 per recovery boiler installation, and confidently projected first-phase sales of over a million dollars per year. That translated to about 100 grand a year in licensing royalties to a guy used to making less than half that annually, and it was a conservative estimate. There were more than two hundred of these boilers operating in North America alone, more than five hundred worldwide.

Weyco's offer was a one-time flat buyout of the patent for $15,000, with a vague hint at a possible future royalty. I don't know what it was, but it wasn't 8% of 500 potential six-figure sales, that's for sure.

Yeah, Tom and Rob were kids, but all Nancy and Byron had to do was a little math. It was a calculated gamble they were making, going with these "young and inexperienced" entrepreneurs, but the potential upside...?

It turned out to be the best bet they would ever make.

Chapter Four
It's Not What, It's Who

"Guys, I have good news and I have bad news," Rob called the as-usual rowdy meeting of Anthony Ross and Associates to order at the local pizza joint. "The good news is Tom and I are going to develop another product. The bad news..."

They were nervous as cats going into this Friday bull session with their business school buddies. They'd kept the name, Anthony-Ross and Associates, though it had pretty much been Rob and Tom figuring out what they were going to do next after the Flow Meter had been relegated to back burner status, and each had gone on.

It was beyond obvious where it was going. All the "Associates" had moved on with their lives and careers as well. They'd gotten good jobs. These guys were colleagues and kindred spirits, but they were first and foremost good friends. Honestly, their "company meetings" had become *guy time*, talking shop, sports, and girls - the lion's share of what most 22-year-old males are interested in. The writing had been on the wall for a while. Still, it was a tad uncomfortable for Tom and Rob to inform the gang of their decision to incorporate their two-man partnership and formally disband the Associates.

It didn't need to be. The Associates cheered, ordered another round, and toasted to the wild success of their pals and the newly formed Anthony-Ross Company.

Now, Tom and Rob were *really* off to the races, right?

Not exactly.

It's true; they did have the top three traits of the Entrepreneur in spades. They were passionate about this invention and the business itself, they most definitely had a spirit of independence and, without families or a mortgage, a high tolerance for risk. They had a good solid plan, they'd done their homework, and they were ready, willing, and able to work tirelessly to succeed. Rob resigned from Weyerhaeuser and Tom graduated from engineering school with a minor in business. All the pieces were in place except for one.

MONEY.

It takes money to make money, the old saying goes. I'm not sure that's true all the time. But in this case, Tom and Rob weren't getting to first base without a healthy chunk of seed capital - like in the neighborhood of $100,000.

The banks turned them down cold. No experience, no collateral, and a refrain that was starting to become familiar: they were just too young. A couple venture capitalists were interested, but their take of the company was so high they'd end up practically owning it, and would surely insist on a hands-on role in its management and direction. This was not an option—not yet, anyway.

There surely had to be a better way to bootstrap this venture and launch a company without giving away the store. Like every entrepreneur must do countless times in not only starting but running their venture, they sat down together with a legal pad and got resourceful.

What do we have? What do we need? Who do we know?

I didn't raise an idiot, and he didn't partner up with an idiot. When my phone rang, I was wondering what had taken them so long.

Now I know what you're thinking, and it wasn't at all so. Tom's older brother was in medical school, and his younger sister was about to start college. Yes, I was a company president, but I wasn't so liquid I could just write a check for a hundred grand and not blink. (I would have done a lot more than blink). I may have been able to do some fancy footwork and pull a healthy chunk from Ella Lee's and my retirement that I'd been funding for thirty years, but I wasn't too keen on doing it.

Fortunately, I also didn't raise a son who would ask. Not that way. What Tom and Rob wanted, and I knew they were sincere in the asking, was my opinion, my experience, my advice.

And that's the phone call every dad in the world cherishes.

I listened carefully as Tom and Rob laid it out. They obviously didn't have to bring me up to speed on Recovery Boilers and port cleaning. I'd been in the paper business for twenty-five years. They'd proven themselves as engineers and as aspiring businessmen. I'd watched them work together since they were sophomores in college.

This was a viable plan, and it was not only correct, it was critical to seek development and production financing. This wasn't something they were going to build in the garage with parts from Home Depot (I don't think there even was a Home Depot in 1982. There wasn't one in my town, anyway). This would entail engineering consultants, fabricating, machining a prototype, and doing it again and again until it was dang near perfect. That costs real money, not to mention the cost of just running a business.

"I see your salaries here," I flipped through the business plan. "Isn't 4500 dollars a bit low?"

"We'll catch up with the first sale," Tom offered.

"Hmmm."

It sounds noble, but it's not the greatest strategic thinking. These things never go fast, not as fast as you think they will, anyway. Unless they were sitting on a pile of personal cash I didn't know about (and they clearly wouldn't be asking for financing advice if they were), they'd have to worry about rent and food and gasoline just like the rest of us. Still, I'd seen enough business plans to be encouraged that Tom and Rob weren't trying to buy themselves a job with other people's money.

After they regaled me with their bank and venture capital misadventures, the conclusion was obvious. "You gotta get investors. It's your only option."

"Yeah, Dad. We just... have no idea how."

"Step One. You need a Board of Advisors."

You can guess who the first one would be.

There is a common misperception among budding entrepreneurs that the investor class in this world is truly only looking for the "Next Big Deal," the quick turnaround, the grand slam homerun. It isn't really so.

Oh, I know the business magazines are brimming over with stories of high-flying start-ups, the geniuses whose venture is so ground-breaking and bullet-proof they're inevitable, and Google's next big acquisition, and on and on. They serve to inspire and push us to press on.

But they rarely tell us the *whole* story. With very, very few exceptions, the question is not *what* an investor is sinking his or her capital into, it's *who*.

Ultimately, they're investing in **you**.

Let's look at Tom and Rob at this moment in their history. They cared. They were passionate about engineering and this business in particular. They knew their stuff. They demonstrated that as engineering students, in the tireless development of their flow meter, and in their respect for and loyalty to Byron, as well as their understanding of what he was designing. That's what sold Byron and Nancy Goodspeed, and convinced them to cast their lots with these two and their un-financed start-up.

These were positive thinking guys. Not unrealistic or pie in the sky, they knew what was ahead of them (well, they thought they did, anyway). They'd done their homework, knew their strengths as well as their shortcomings, and set a high but attainable bar for success. It was obvious that these two would persist until they attained that bar, and jumped right over it.

What would ultimately convince Nancy and Byron that their best bet was in these two wet-behind-ears entrepreneurs—they were twenty-two for heavens sake!—was their honesty and their obvious integrity. They didn't pretend to be any more than they were when they presented their business proposal. They answered each one of Nancy's tough questions honestly, even when it didn't exactly make them look like two guys about to be on the cover of one of those magazines. Both of them were completely sincere in wishing Byron the best if he indeed decided to go with selling his invention outright to the big company.

It was not exactly the easiest situation when Byron asked to be a full-time partner. It would have never worked, and the guys knew it. Byron was a first class inventor, but he was also that lovable, "nutty professor type," not a businessman. This would have been a disaster for both him and the company. But Byron was also a sensitive man who took things personally. His request had to be handled delicately. Rob and Tom gently pointed out that his talents were in the workshop, not in a sales meeting. And honestly, they didn't have the money to pay him. Happily, he agreed.

Passion. Optimism. Honesty. Integrity. Hard Work. Tenacity. It was these qualities that had gotten Tom and Rob this far, and these were the qualities they would need for the next step - financing their company.

Let me say it again. It's not what, it's who.

Their Business Plan called for $75,000. The ideal situation was a group of five investors who could also serve as advisors, or mentors, as well as their Board of Directors. Each board member would receive a 2% interest in the company in exchange for an investment of $2000. In addition, each board member would pledge a loan of up to $13,000. This would give them the working capital to start the business, and leave Tom and Rob with 90% ownership.

The perfect investor, from their point of view, was first off someone who was willing and able to invest the money. Secondly, Tom and Rob were both smart and humble enough to have learned from their first go with the Flow Meter. Now they knew, despite their giftedness as engineers, there was a whole lot *they didn't know*. This would end up making all the difference, in my view. Their Board of Directors was a true Board of *Advisers*, men who had been in business for many more years than the two of them had been alive. Finally, because of their youth and inexperience, it was obvious to both Tom and Rob, the investor would surely need to know them personally.

They found four: myself, a prominent Portland attorney, the president of a Savings and Loan, and a manufacturing representative. All the critical areas of a start-up business were covered with a seasoned advisor: executive, legal, banking, and sales. Between us, we had over 120 years of experience in our fields. That still left them one investor and $15,000 short. I would eventually raise my share to 4% of the company, and anteed up accordingly.

Yes, I had known these Advisers a while. Each knew Tom, and had watched him grow up, and they'd met Rob. They did not jump in out of any obligation to me, and I assure you, I wouldn't have asked. Please let me hammer this point again, as it is critical to anyone seeking to understand the thinking of a potential investor:

It's not what, it's <u>who</u>.

I didn't do the work for them, didn't set up meetings, or even make the calls. I gave them a list of potential candidates, and that was it. I wasn't about to pressure my friends into a business investment. They could judge for themselves whether the venture and the principals were worth the risk.

Tom and Rob sought the men out, explained their product and their plan in detail, looked them in the eye, and asked for the investment. Their integrity and honesty were obvious, and it was clear they would put in the sweat.

It's tough to fake that, and trust me, people who have been slugging it out in the marketplace for 30+ years can smell the opposite a mile away. These guys weren't fools, and neither was I. None of us, including the loving dad, was about to throw fifteen grand into the wind, hoping my son and his buddy's little venture might succeed.

I gotta be careful here being Tom's dad and all, but there's one thing you need to know. I'm really not a softie. I knew this business, understood their offering, and saw it could work. But with my years, I also knew the chances of failure were equal to if not greater than success. There are just too many unknowns out there and they really were just kids who didn't have a clue what they were really getting into, but we went for it anyway. Why?

Tom and Rob sold us, and I mean that word in its highest sense, with their enthusiasm, the hard work they'd already done, a pretty good idea, and a clear honesty and candor. Lastly, and I think most importantly, they were sincere in seeking us out for more than just our money.

This is important. Please take this point, because we need to understand the mindset of an investor if we ever hope to secure his investment.

None of us joined this Board thinking we were investing in the next Google. To the contrary. Again, we all knew what a high risk venture this really was, much better than the principals, candidly. Two things convinced us to roll up our sleeves and open up our checkbook: who these young men were *as people*, and the sheer "juice" of being in the game.

This is my last point in this chapter. There is very little in this life more satisfying than seeing an idea, something that started as a thought, come to life, and *succeed*, and know that you had something to do with that. It's why we love sports so much. It's ultimately why business people *choose* business. At the end of it all, it's why we love our country so much. We've got skin in this game!

The vast majority of people, *investors*, want a lot more than money. They want to be in the game. They want to be part of something bigger than themselves, and they want to put *more* of themselves than just their dough into that something. They want to invest their talents, their wisdom, and their experience and - yes - their money in something and *somebody* they believe in...and watch it fly. No matter how great the offering, they're not going to get in that game if they're not comfortable with the people playing it.

It's not what, folks. It's who.

Chapter Five
People Need People

Jim Holst stopped mid-stride as he rounded the corner of the hallway in Kristen Square, the small office park in Beaverton. Jim was a good friend to Rob and Tom, just decided he'd drop by on his way to work to check out the guys' new digs, and wish the just-incorporated Anthony-Ross Company well.

There stood Tom, outside their new office, with no apparent reason or purpose. It looked like he'd been there for a while.

"Tom… What are you doing?"

"Oh. Hey, Jim. Just waiting for Rob to get off the phone."

"Is everything all right?"

"Sure, sure. It's just a sales call."

"Okay. Do you, uh, step outside for every sales call, Tom?"

"Oh yeah."

Well, it was a tiny office. 10X10. The simple fact was neither could stand the other in the room when he had to make a sales call. Tom explained it to his friend as needing the quiet. Certainly, they didn't want to let on to the person at the other end of that phone that the "Anthony-Ross Complex" consisted of two desks put together to double as a drafting table and sometimes lunch counter, one filing cabinet, a fake fern and one phone, with the founding partners working 12+ hours a day about 36 inches apart. It's a plausible explanation, but not entirely accurate.

Each was just that self-conscious. They were so new to this, and had no real experience in sales beyond selling World's Finest Chocolate door–to-door for their high schools. They were flying by the seat of their pants, cold-calling a list of paper industry contacts, and not faring all that well.

Most times, it seemed, they'd have old information, or they'd get the wrong person on the phone. They'd rehearsed their pitch again and again, but it never seemed to come out right. More often than not, they would get a question from the prospect they just couldn't answer.

Do I even have to tell you that the orders weren't flying in? They weren't even crawling in. Besides, there were more pressing matters in front of them. Though these were two positive-thinking and persistent guys absolutely oozing the rest of the 12 Steps of Success, it was becoming clearer to them by the day. Nobody gets very far in this world all by himself. We need others to help us realize our dreams. Tom and Rob were no exception.

It wasn't just a matter of making cold calls and selling port cleaners. There was a lot to do. Besides simply organizing the business, which is *never* simple, by the way, the APC itself would have to be machined and made into a prototype, tested, modified, tested again, and then the whole process repeated. That's what engineering is. Before they could get to the engineering, they needed to file Byron's patent, which should have been a simple matter of routine.

It wasn't.

Weyerhaeuser claimed the rights to the patent, and informed Anthony-Ross that they could not file. This was a bombshell to us all. If they couldn't secure the patent, the game was over before it even began. We couldn't wave this one away. Weyerhaeuser had a legitimate claim.

Byron Goodspeed was a Weyerhaeuser employee. From their point of view, he developed the port cleaner on their company property, using materials from their shop, tested on their boiler, on company time. In their mind, the APC belonged to them.

Now, this is a long-running intellectual property debate. All of the above is mostly accurate, if you discount Byron's own intellect and life experience as a tinkerer and the countless hours in his own garage. Let's remember, with all due respect to Weyerhaeuser, without Byron and his unique invention, there's nothing for anyone to patent.

There was certainly nothing nefarious in his developing this invention on "company time." Ultimately, he was trying to solve a problem for that company. Was it his fault Weyco didn't sufficiently value this solution and want to share in its future? Didn't he have the right to seek another market, for what the company agreed, was ultimately his intellectual property?

These are age-old questions of pure logic, but you can never dismiss the emotional factor in business.

Weyerhaeuser didn't exactly send fruit baskets, cards, and champagne when Anthony-Ross opened their tiny office. They were a little miffed about the outcome of the negotiations with Byron, perhaps a tad embarrassed, and they were digging in for a fight. The stage was being set for a legal battle, a battle a major corporation is well-funded to fight. This little two-desk/one-phone start-up could not possibly afford to do so.

Somebody was going to have to mediate here, or the Anthony-Ross Company would never get off the ground. What was to become the industry's gold standard for this critical component in the paper-making process might never come to be.

This was shaping up to be a classic Lose/Lose for all.

There's an old saw that nobody likes lawyers, *until they need one.* The guys needed one. Enter patent attorney John Deolett. I had dealt with John when I was at Publishers Paper, and never had a bad experience with him. He'd recently left a very large firm, and hung out the shingle to open his own practice. He was inspired by Tom and Rob's pluck and youthful tenacity, and all too happy to take them on as a new client.

John was not the stereotypical hard-charging, win-at-all-costs lawyer. He was a gentle, soft-spoken, deeply spiritual man whose approach was to seek a win/win in every legal or business situation. He was a born mediator, with twenty-five years of patent law under his belt, more than up to the challenge of this sticky impasse.

John could see Weyerhaeuser's point of view, and told us from the get-go they had a case. He could also see two very sincere young engineers who weren't out poaching an invention from one of Weyco's employees to make a quick buck. They were trying to build something that everyone - Weyerhaeuser included - could benefit mightily from.

It's important to emphasize, Weyerhaeuser wasn't a bunch of ill-willed corporate bad guys exacting revenge on this little start-up, or even their own employee. They had no interest in tying this up in the courts, either, but they felt like they owned the port cleaner that Anthony-Ross was trying to patent for Byron, who still worked there. (Tom and Rob insisted he stay while they built their company, as did his wife!).

It was a good idea to bring John into this. It was a delicate negotiation. It took several months but, in the end, logic and good will prevailed. Byron would own the patent on the Automatic Port Cleaner, Anthony-Ross would license it, Weyerhaeuser would keep the "shop rights" to that patent (they could build and install their own APC without licensing), and all the test data remained proprietary to the company.

The patent was filed and granted. Anthony-Ross and Weyerhaeuser shook hands, signed the agreement, and got back to work. It looked like a Happily Ever After, Win/Win for both sides.

We would find out soon enough, however, that it really wasn't.

"Good morning, thank you for calling the Anthony-Ross Company," came the pleasant and professional voice of a well-trained receptionist. "How may I direct your call?"

Many people have closets that are larger than the original 100 square foot nerve center of the Anthony-Ross Company. To call their office Spartan and efficient is being kind, but it served the purposes of a start-up just fine. On top of the bargain basement rent they were paying, one perk made it the best deal in town. With their lease came Shared Secretarial Service, a receptionist and secretarial service shared by the building's other tenants.

Now this is huge. They certainly couldn't afford to hire any employees, and this took a tremendous burden off them time-wise. More than that, image may not be everything, but in the early stages of a start-up, *it's a lot*. Something seemingly as insignificant as a receptionist answering your line with your company's name can make all the difference in the world.

It's funny now, recalling Rob and Tom both counting the appropriate seconds before picking up, putting the caller "on hold" by putting their hand over the phone, or "transferring" them to the Engineering Department by silently passing the receiver across the 36 inches separating them. The last image they wanted to convey was that of two 22-year-olds right out of college making it up as they went along.

There was more to it than simple appearances. Nobody can do everything, and do it all well. The sheer volume of the engineering and sales work in front of them didn't leave much time for writing letters, doing corporate taxes, organizing, and filing and taking care of the gazillion details that go with running a business. Besides, Rob was not a detail guy. Tom *was*, but his expertise (and passion) was with *engineering* details. He had little or no experience in the paperwork side of things, and certainly no passion for it. As well spoken as he was, Tom couldn't spell his way out of a paper bag.

Shared Secretarial Service turned out to be more than a secretarial service. It was a godsend.

Life had taken more than its share of tough turns for Paula Zimmerman by 1982. Only 29, a single mother of two girls, she was going through a terrible divorce after a difficult ten-year marriage to a man losing his battle with alcohol addiction. She needed a job, and got hired on by the secretarial service in Rob and Tom's building.

Paula was competent and capable, but her spirits were not exactly sky-high when she arrived for her first day on the job at Kristen Square. Her confidence and self-esteem were hovering near zero after this divorce and the very difficult time she was having on her own. With a very uncertain future, she feared for her daughters, and herself, quite honestly. This was not at all a career move; this was more like a "temp" job, buying her some breathing room to figure out what to do next.

The first ones she met were the "boys down the hall." Her first reaction was laughter. "I mean, here are these very sincere, and *very young* guys, trying to look older and more distinguished by wearing suits to the office every day, which I thought made them look even younger. I remember taking calls from these great big companies, acting as a private secretary, 'getting them out of a meeting,' then counting how long it would be before one would step out in the hall while the other talked. You just couldn't help but pull for these guys."

Paula looked after the fledgling little start-up, helping them not only maintain a more seasoned and professional image, but anticipating and solving problems before Tom and Rob even knew they *were* problems. In her second year, she could clearly see one major hurdle. These guys needed a computer, a *real* computer, and it was equally clear they couldn't afford one.

Again, we need to look at the timeframe. In the early 80s, there was no Dell or Gateway or any of the other hundreds of high-functioning computers available to any of us now for a few hundred bucks. Tom and Rob needed a lot more than a word processor. This was an engineering firm after all, yet they didn't have a computer. The type they would need cost nearly $10,000 in 1983. They could easily justify the expense, but the funds just were not there.

Paula was in a terrific position to help them. Her boss, the owner of Shared Secretarial Service, was an entrepreneur with several businesses, and took an instant liking to Tom and Rob. One of his enterprises was selling high-end computers to the business world, and he just happened to have one with the exact specifications the guys would need. It didn't take Paula five minutes to talk him into selling that computer to them - at his cost - with very flexible financing options. It saved the guys thousands. With no bank credit line, it was the only way they could have possibly gotten this crucial tool.

For the next four years, that computer was running a minimum of 12 hours a day, six days a week, and then some, all because of one conversation, one set of watchful and caring eyes, and Paula Zimmerman's willingness to go to bat for these two "very sincere" guys, struggling against all odds to make a go of it. And it made all the difference in the world.

Later, when the company was viable and hiring engineers, they had wisely hired Paula full time. She could see 100 square feet would never do. Paula's entrepreneur boss was also a commercial real estate broker, who had a substantial office-industrial space he'd not been able to rent for a couple years. He essentially gave it to Anthony-Ross.

All this, and much more, from a woman who was working for a secretarial service that just happened to have this building for a client. Why, then? Why would she keep a lookout for the well-being of these two kids and their fledgling little start-up? Just because they were sincere?

Maybe, but I suspect there's something more, and it's why I linger on this point.

Author/Speaker Andy Andrews reminds us to never forget a simple fact in business and human relations. "That woman answering the phones is not your receptionist, she's the Executive in Charge of First Impressions. And if you think that's not important, watch what happens when she's not there."

Paula wouldn't be on the Anthony-Ross payroll for nearly three years, and yet those little stories are only two of literally scores of examples of her going above and beyond the call of her job description for Shared Secretarial Service, answering the client's phones, and typing a letter or two.

Tom and Rob recognized that Paula was far more than the woman answering the phone; she was an ally, a teammate. They asked questions, and listened to her answers. They sought her counsel on everything from their business letters to their cold calling. They respected her, and it was genuine.

These simple acts, repeated daily, were more valuable than any paycheck or benefit Paula Zimmerman needed, after years of emotional pain and struggle. What Paula needed most was her self-esteem and her self-respect back.

She would stay with the company for their entire time as founding partners, and another 14 years after each left. She was indeed the Department of First Impressions, and a whole lot more to the Anthony-Ross Company. But Paula was more than an employee, she was part of our family. Tom and Rob (and I) watched her children grow up. Watched her fall in love again and re-marry.

"Meeting Tom and Rob was the first step in my recovery from 10 very hard years," Paula remembers now, with more than a little emotion. "They encouraged me and guided me without even knowing it. They reminded me I was valuable - a good person and a good Mom. I needed someone to tell me that, to tell me I was going to be okay."

Companies need employees. Employees need a job. That's how business works, that's how economies work. Let's never forget that this journey is about a lot more than making money and building businesses and growing economies...

It's about making the world work. The fundamental truth of business is the same as the fundamental truth of human life, to quote an old song...

People Need People.

Chapter Six
"Sales Drives the Company..."

"Yeah," Tom would laugh at and add to Rob's frequent proclamation. "Drive the company *into the ground* or maybe *off a cliff.*"

Whichever metaphor Tom would have picked, it would have fit the first year of the Sales Department of the Anthony-Ross Company. "Here we go again," Tom thought to himself, as their pitch to Boise Cascade twelve months in began to crater.

Rob's presentation wasn't exactly a barn burner. It was more like a technical presentation to a roomful of engineers, filled with irrelevant detail and data, not that Tom's presentations were any better. The problem is the men at Boise weren't engineers. They were executives who were fidgeting, glancing, some actually *staring* at their watches. One was literally asleep. Tom was signaling to Rob with his eyes to wrap it up. This one was going nowhere.

The guys' approach was clearly not working. They had a really great invention, with an immediate application to save these paper mills all kinds of money and headache. But the fact remained. They'd incorporated a year before, and had not taken a single order.

The money was running out. $75,000 seemed like a whole lot of dough to two 23 year olds in 1982, but I knew it wasn't enough. As a board member and the largest shareholder, I made my feelings known on this, but I did respect their refusal to take on too much debt. Still, even with the cheap cracker box office and the sub-minimum-wage salaries Tom and Rob were paying themselves, engineering, consulting, legal, and fabricating costs were taking their toll on the company's bank account. The well was quickly running dry.

Why? What could the problem possibly be? We've discussed their youth and inexperience, but they were a year older now. As a sidelight to that point, they had opted to grow moustaches to enhance the perception of wisdom and experience that much more. I will reserve comment on how well that worked, though I think the early results speak for themselves.

There was obviously a bigger problem here, and it was more than youth and inexperience at sales.

It goes back to the Data.

Dr. Chuck Denham, Advanced Leadership Fellow of Harvard University, teaches a four-letter acronym for establishing any successful business relationship: **CEMO.** You can call it your "pitch." The four elements that must be present and must be compelling to the prospect. Essentially, if you don't have a good, strong CEMO, you won't get the order. So what in the world is a CEMO?

C.E.M.O. = Claim+Evidence+Method+Offering.

The CLAIM is the value proposition, the essence of what you're selling, the reason someone wants to do business with you. The Evidence is the proof of that claim -that you can actually do what you say you can do. The Method is how you will actually do it. The Offering is the deal: I will do this for you, for the sum we agree upon. This is the foundation of sales.

Let's look at the Anthony-Ross CEMO with a quarter century's worth of hindsight. Their Claim to Boise Cascade and the other prospects, rookie presentation aside, truly was an attention-getter: Our product will dramatically improve your efficiency and save you hundreds of thousands of dollars annually in energy costs. That will get anybody's attention. Their Method was the Automatic Port

Cleaning System, which they would customize, build, and install on that boiler. The offering was to sell them this system at a price that was less than the first year's energy savings.

Win/Win, right?

Well, you don't have to be the sharpest tool in the shed to see one of the four elements of the CEMO is missing here: The Evidence. The Proof. It's the most critical of them all. Without the Proof, all the new moustaches, patents, engineering degrees, and sincerity didn't add up to a hill of wet paper pulp. If they couldn't prove it, they weren't going to get any orders.

And they couldn't prove it.

When Anthony-Ross settled Byron's patent situation with Weyerhaeuser, it seemed like a textbook Win/Win. Anthony-Ross got the legal clearance to produce and sell the APC, and Weyerhaeuser got the "shop rights" to produce the system themselves, in-house, for no royalty payment. You will recall there was one more caveat, and oh boy *was* it a caveat. All the results and test data of Weyerhaeuser's working model remained proprietary information - *a corporate secret*! Anthony-Ross could not access or share the results data of the only working APC system in existence. If they couldn't access the data, they couldn't prove their claim. If they couldn't prove their claim, who was gonna buy it?

The answer was obvious in the Boise Cascade presentation, and in a whole slew of other meetings with the same result: *Nobody*. The boys were sunk before their pitch even began.

Now I don't want to give you the wrong impression. There was no oversight here. This little caveat didn't just slip by John Deleott and the Board when we settled with Weyco. They just weren't going budge on this point, and you couldn't blame them. Releasing test data on their boiler would essentially reveal their process, their trade secrets to the world. It was the Dealbreaker, and John knew it. The most important thing for Anthony-Ross at that point was to get that patent, which they did. This lack of data, however, would be more than just a hill to climb; it was turning out to be Mt. Everest.

You might be asking, then, why didn't they just go ahead and produce the APCs and let the mills take them on a "try-before-you-buy" basis? Two problems there: first off, no two boiler systems were the same. Each would have to be custom designed for each prospect. There would be no way to mass-produce the exact same system for multiple boilers. Second, the cost. The company's entire seed financing investment of $75,000 wouldn't cover the production of one system and its installation.

To adopt that strategy wouldn't be entrepreneurial risk-taking; it would be foolishness and simply out of reach for a small start-up. It was never considered.

As Tom and Rob trudged across the Boise parking lot to their car after the meeting, the writing was on the wall for the Anthony-Ross Co.—in bold, indelible ink.

"We gotta make something happen, Rob, or we're done."

"I know, Tom. I know."

They were eventually able to take one important step. The mill at Wauna agreed to put in a demonstration unit so they could evaluate the equipment. This was a start, and would actually be the turning point of the company. Until that day arrived, they were going to have to get out there and sell this thing. But first, they were going to have to learn how.

The Piper Cherokee approached the tower-less airfield some-where in the middle of Montana. Vic Risley feathered the controls, announced himself to any nearby air traffic, and set her down like a pro. He taxied to an empty out-building with a station wagon he'd arranged to have waiting there, and shut the engine down.

"This is gonna be fun," Vic smiled at his only passenger, Rob Anthony.

"How do you want me to do this? With you, I mean?"

"Just like you always do. No different."

"Oh. Great," Rob managed, as he climbed out onto the wing-step.

Vic Risley could have been a movie star if he'd chosen that route. Six foot five, handsome, born to wear a good suit. Vic was one of the original four investors in Anthony-Ross and on our board as the "sales guy," which is rather like having Michael Jordan on your board as the "sports guy." It doesn't begin to describe who he is or what he has accomplished in his field.

We have an aversion, in this country, to sales people. Now this is a strange aversion, as sales is the absolute cornerstone of any business. It's junior high school economics. You can have the greatest goods or services on the planet, but if you're not *selling* those goods and services, you're not long for the business world.

Hollywood hasn't helped. Salespeople are generally stereotyped in TV and movies as slightly shady, less than scrupulous folk. A lot of people, myself included at times, profess a strong dislike for "being sold." Many avoid it and salespeople whenever humanly possible.

They never met Vic. I'd known him for twenty years, since he first called on me as a purchasing manager. He ran so counter to the "salesman" stereotype, I would drop whatever I was doing when he showed up, just to sit and talk with this personable, well-spoken, very sincere guy. I can't think of one other salesperson for whom I would ever do that. Judging by his spectacular success rate, I wasn't the only purchasing manager who felt that way. Vic Risley truly had the master's touch when it came to personal relationships and sales.

"They're really struggling, aren't they?" he'd asked me after a board meeting at my house one evening.

"They really are, Vic. This test data thing is killing 'em."

"I wish I could help with that, but I wouldn't understand it even if I saw it."

"Well, without that data, they're gonna have to do some job of selling, Vic."

"Now <u>that</u>," Vic grinned, "I can help with."

Vic listened patiently as Rob presented to the mill manager, never speaking once. He didn't comment on Rob's performance heading back to the plane without an order, either. They next flew to a mill in Eastern Washington, where Vic whispered calmly and with no bravado to Rob as they entered the conference room, "Watch me this time."

Within thirty minutes, Vic had the vice president's card and next year's purchasing schedule, as well as the names and ages of all his kids and what sports they played. "We'll do the follow up before they do their annual budgeting," Vic said as casually as if he were talking about the weather as they headed back to the airport. "He's a good prospect. You'll get the order."

"If I was the beginning cellist," Rob laughs now, "Vic was Yo-Yo Ma. I was just speechless, watching a master at the top of his profession."

Vic didn't spend that half hour dazzling the vice president with a Power-point presentation or a 'dynamic' pitch. He asked the right questions, did more listening than talking, and *really listened.* As Rob would remember 25 years later, Vic wasn't "selling." He was "serving." And he was sincere. It wasn't an act; he really felt that way.

There are some great actors out there, but nearly all of them are on stage or on screen. Contrary to the tired stereotypical slick and disingenuous salesman, sincerity is the hardest thing of all to fake. If you ain't got it, people know. Human beings, especially those human beings in the marketplace every day, are just wired up with the appropriate built-in radar. We know when we're being put on - being "sold." We also have the radar for when people are for real.

This is not a discourse on selling. This is common sense, and is the foundation of all business. The sales courses call it "building rapport," which it certainly is, but this should be lingered on longer than any other of the Twelve Steps. Truly, without this one, you won't even get to the other 11. The engine that drives sales and business and economies ultimately is this First Step:

I CARE.

What made Rob's jaw hit the floor, watching Vic, was just how little he employed facts, figures, and the Claim of the Anthony-Ross CEMO - the things on which Rob had concentrated his approach. No formula or visible "technique," Vic spent the majority of that half-hour meeting *listening*, not pitching. His manner was that of a man truly comfortable in his own skin, knowledgeable about the business, relaxed, not trying too hard, and genuinely wanting to make this man's business and life that much better.

*Who doesn't want **that** person in his office?*

This vice president, in thirty minutes, went from cool and distant to warm and friendly. Facts and figures won't do that. A new friendship will.

It's the same reason I would end meetings or get off the phone when my secretary would tell me "Salesman Vic Risley" was in the building. I don't remember our first meeting, but I am certain it was nearly identical to the one Rob watched as a protégé. I gave Vic all sorts of orders over the course of 20-something years, both of us benefited mightily as a result of his selling and my buying. What mattered most to me, and why I always went back to Vic, was our friendship - born out of our business together.

The guys had more or less by default divided the two major areas of focus between them: Tom would focus on Operations, Rob on Sales. It was a natural division. Tom was more the detail guy, Rob loved talking to people. By no means does that make one a natural at selling, and there was a lot Rob had to learn about sales, for sure. By watching Vic in action, he learned that first and foremost, sales is all about the relationship. If you're going to get that, **you gotta care.**

There is another old Chinese proverb. *When the student is ready, the teacher will appear.* This idea was lived out in Vic's mentoring Rob in sales. Vic became a coach to Rob, but the relationship grew far deeper than either might have guessed that first day. Next to Tom and the woman who became his wife, Vic became one of Rob's closest friends.

There is something special about passing on the wisdom of your years and experience to the next generation, especially when they are eager to learn from you! Rob was motivated and eager. He could see the end of the line for the Anthony-Ross Company if he didn't make a sale, and soon. More than that, Rob was a competitor and didn't like losing at anything. To him, every bad presentation or even a good presentation with no order or follow-up felt like a loss, and Vic's ease and comfort at this game was more than obvious. Whatever he was doing, Rob wanted to know!

For the better part of a year, they traveled together regularly. Like a flight instructor and a student pilot, Vic was more and more giving Rob the shtick in their meetings, preparing him. Vic didn't know it yet, but he and his protégé were soon to have an exclusive agreement with the Anthony-Ross Company to represent them on the West Coast. Still, there was a lot more going on here than a sales training process. A lasting bond was being formed on the long lonely highways and cross-country single engine plane flights; a bond that went far beyond the mentor and his apprentice, or just simply working together.

Vic Risley was an atheist. Not an angry, God-hating zealot, he had simply come to the intellectual conclusion that there was no God. Now this, of course, was a shock at first to the young, evangelical Christian that was Rob Anthony. But once that shock wore off, it became less a point of contention and more a point of fascination - and challenge to him. Rob wanted to know precisely *how* one comes to that conclusion. A bad growing up experience? Nope. Had God let Vic down in some way, somewhere along his life? A tragedy or a shattered dream or unanswered prayer? Had he renounced an earlier faith? No. None of the above. It was just a rational choice. No emotion seemed to be wrapped up in it at all. He wasn't defensive or antagonistic. As I said, you couldn't find a nicer guy anywhere than Vic Risley.

But he *was* curious. He had as many questions for Rob as Rob had for him. I don't know if you've ever driven from Portland to Montana, or flown a single engine plane deep into Canada, but there are a lot of wide-open spaces and vast stretches of nothing for hours out there, to fully explore and talk out any topic. This became as much a basis for their friendship as Rob's sales training. It was a genuine debate and running Q&A between a born-again Christian and an atheist, and neither seemed to ever tire of it.

No, Rob never "converted" Vic. For a while, he quietly wondered if he'd failed by not doing so. Was the Creator was giving him a test or an early ministry opportunity by putting him alongside an avowed atheist for long stretches of time? Maybe he should have been more forceful and proactive? Then again, doing that might have ended this mentoring relationship, or even their friendship, which the young man was growing to cherish more every single sales call, every car or plane trip.

With the benefit of time, Rob sees it much clearer now. He would not be selling the Anthony-Ross APC forever. One day, he would be preaching to his own congregation as a senior pastor. If you ask him now, he will mention his seminary training as a necessary step for this calling. What he learned as a partner in Anthony-Ross, especially what he learned from Vic, was the real preparation.

"Vic taught me sales, which, at the end of the day, is all preaching really is," Rob laughs, before turning serious. "But what he really taught me was kindness and compassion. Talk less, listen more, and respect other points of view."

Only with the perspective of years has Rob come to realize that Vic Risley wasn't just preparing the twenty-three year old entrepreneur for success in business, he was preparing him for his life's work and ultimate purpose.

The student was ready, and the teacher indeed appeared.

Chapter Seven
Breakthrough

"So," the Mill Manager in Louisiana leaned back in his chair and positively snarled at Rob, "How much you wantin' to soak me for?"

"Excuse me?" Rob spluttered in response.

"How much is this dog and pony show you're sellin' cost, boy? Not that I'm buying, I just want to know."

Rob wanted to laugh, then started to get mad, then quickly composed himself. In all his sales calls with Vic, he'd never encountered a response to his presentation quite like this. Now here he was flying solo, presenting the Anthony-Ross APC to a paper mill in a part of the country this Oregon boy couldn't begin to comprehend. He was having a heck of a time discerning any English words in the deep Cajun accent, for starters, and now here was one rattlesnake-mean guy demanding answers he didn't have yet.

"Well, it's not like we have a one size fits all, we need to..."

"Just tell me how much, son!"

"...we need to examine the boiler," Rob continued. "Take some measurements, do some temperature and pressure testing, determine how many units you need."

"I don't like salesmen. You come waltzin' in here, telling me what you think I want to hear so you can soak me for a big fat check for your gizmo. Is that what you really think is gonna happen?"

Let's FREEZE FRAME this scene right here.

Anthony-Ross was coming up on 18 months without a sale. Running on fumes financially, I wouldn't say their youthful exuberance and confidence had faded into despair and surrender, but Rob and Tom were certainly coming to grips with reality. All us 'seasoned veterans' on the Board knew very well that their initial projection of a sale in the first few months was optimistic, at best. Now, a year and a half later, they had prospects, they had leads, they even had demonstration units running at several mills, but they didn't have a single closed deal. They were running out of time, and they were running out of dough.

Think about this, now. 18 months. Not a dollar of revenue. They'd engaged Industrial Machine, a shop in Kelso to produce the demonstration unit and a model for their pitch meetings, and the shop had been amazingly generous in their terms, spotting a huge opportunity if these guys went the distance with this thing. Still, there was cost to running this little operation. Their cracker box office wasn't free, nor was their cracker box apartment. They had utilities, a phone line, engineering and consulting fees, a fax machine, and a new computer that may have been "at cost," but that didn't make it cheap by most standards. There were quarterly taxes, sub-minimum wage salaries for themselves just so they could eat and keep their lights on, plane fare to Texas, Louisiana, Arkansas, and anywhere else that might have a paper mill close by. Then there was gasoline, pencil sharpeners, waste paper baskets, coffee, coffee, and more coffee.

I think you get the idea. The realities that were dawning on them more than any other were how slow this would actually go, and how fast $75K would fly out of the company checking account. I am hammering this point for one very simple reason. This wasn't failure. This was the time-honored Process of Starting a Business:

Great Idea, followed by a Plan, followed by Optimistic and Enthusiastic Start-up, followed by a Good Old Fashioned Fanny-Whooping by the marketplace.

Conventional wisdom holds that most start-ups don't start making money until their second or third year. By that measure, the guys were right on schedule. Their great idea, plan, and optimistic and enthusiastic start-up now had them in the inevitable fanny-whooping phase. They may have taken some comfort in that, but not much.

Their risk was real.

Remember how they structured the financing of this company; the true "investment" cash put in by the shareholders was only $10,000. The remainder came in the form of four personal *loans*. If they failed, they weren't going to be able to just shrug it off, chalk it up to a little bad luck, and walk away. They'd made the commitment to go for it, and acted on that commitment by licensing Byron's patent and hanging out the Anthony-Ross shingle. They were in the game for real, and that meant they were on the hook for $65,000: legally, contractually, and morally.

Quitting just was not an option.

Still, youth, inexperience, lack of test data, lack of capital. That's a lot to overcome. After 18 months of *zip-zero-nada*, more than enough for most people to call it a day, they didn't throw in the towel. They persisted. And why wouldn't they? They believed in their mission, they were obligated to pay back the loans, and most tellingly, they felt morally bound to Byron, who'd entrusted his life's work to them.

"Common sense probably should have told us this was impossible, the odds against us were just too great," Tom recalls this very difficult period now. "But if we'd quit, I don't think we could have faced Byron again. And besides, I knew eventually, our luck had to change."

There was only one course left to them, and they took it: *massive action*. Tom and Rob shifted their focus from selling a unit to becoming the de facto industry experts on recovery boilers and port cleaning.

Now to do that, they would have to positively re-immerse themselves into every facet and detail of not only their product, but also the heating process itself. To throw away everything they thought they knew, and learn it fresh again, as though for the very first time. They designed their own crash course, pored over every piece of technical data they could find, visited every paper mill in the Northwest, whether they were calling on them or not, and got to know their boiler up close and personal. They drove the millwrights crazy with their endless questions, practically lived at the Industrial Machine shop in Kelso, tearing the APC apart and putting it back together again.

But there was one more thing.

Rob Anthony was a charming and engaging young man. His boyhood stammer was barely a memory now. He could cite the specs and the data on the APC all day long. You know what? When it comes to **sales**, all that doesn't add up to *squat*. Tom was right in his earlier joke. Sales will drive the company straight into the ground... *if it isn't done right.*

His job heading up sales for the fledgling Anthony-Ross Company was not an afterthought, and neither is the sales department in any venture. Winning smiles, neat appearances, and great interpersonal skills barely scratch the surface. Until Rob spent a year with a master at the art and science of selling, he didn't really understand that. Now, after an intensive on the job apprenticeship with Vic Risley, he did. Vic taught him in his words and his actions that selling comes down really to just three things: establishing a decent rapport with the person you wish to serve, being able to read the wants and needs of that person, and the discernment to act accordingly.

This is sales. Just like engineering, mastering it takes time, study, and practice.

#7. I Never Stop Learning.

Now let's go back to Louisiana and unfreeze the picture. The hostile Mill Manager stares at the young salesman, arms folded, waiting for an answer. One of the paper industry's recognized experts on recovery boilers and port cleaners, and a Vic Risley-trained salesman to boot, decide it's time to stand up to this guy.

"Sir, I honestly can't tell you the cost yet. Every system is a custom design and installation. I'll need to assess and measure your boiler before I even know how many units to install."

"The way I see it," the crusty old guy drawled, "If it ain't broke, you don't fix it. And the way we do it ain't broke." (*Sound familiar?*)

Rob could see this was a one-way conversation. He put the company literature and demonstration unit back in his briefcase.

"The fact is, sir, the way you do it is not the most efficient way, and it's costing you hundreds of thousands of dollars per year. If that's the way you want to continue maintaining your boiler, I guess we're done here." He clicked the briefcase shut. "And one last thing. I'm not in the business of soaking people. I'm in the business of **serving** them."

"Son, you didn't fly all the way across the country just to turn tail and go home, did ya?"

"I came here to do business, not be insulted. If you're not interested in what I have to say, I know your competitors are. Have a nice day."

"Hold it, young man." Rob was halfway out the door when the Mill Manager stopped him. He grinned suddenly, and nodded. "I like you. I like anybody with fire in his belly. Get back in here and show me that thing again, would ya?"

Rob was at the man's house for dinner that night, eating his first deep-fried turkey, along with what seemed his entire extended family and half of the small town they were in. A friendship grew out of that confrontation. The mill manager truly admired Rob, not only for believing in what he was doing, but for being man enough to stand up to him. My guess is his view of salespeople was altered significantly.

Still, he didn't buy a port cleaner. Not yet, anyway.

All good relations aside, installation fees to install demonstration units would not keep this company alive. The writing was on the wall. If they couldn't make a sale, Anthony-Ross was done, and they would be done soon, unless something happened.

A couple days later, Rob measured the boiler and installed a demonstration unit at the Temple East-Tex mill in Orange, Texas. My friend Fletcher Smith was a manufacturer's representative in the South, and Anthony-Ross had engaged him, similar in manner to our arrangement with Vic Risley. Fletcher was an excellent salesman himself. His presentation to the mill was compelling enough for them to send for Rob to make a formal proposal.

Rob took Fletcher's tee-up, and made the presentation of his life. In his sports-oriented mind, this truly was the bottom of the ninth for his company, late in the fourth quarter, the 18th hole… whatever sports analogy you want to use. No mulligan here. His team was in the hole and they needed a break. Like, right now.

It wasn't flashy, loaded with bells and whistles, or high-pressure. It was the perfect combination of his genuine enthusiasm, a great product, and just being *real*. Vic Risley had made this perfect combination look so easy. It wasn't, but Vic's young protégé was at the top of his game now. Rob knocked the pitch and demonstration out of the park.

He sat back in his airplane seat as the plane took off for Portland. He'd done the best he possibly could. Still, he and Tom had been disappointed before, to put it mildly. There was no more certainty they would get this order, either.

It was a bright sunny day in May when Byron Goodspeed and his wife Nancy entered the offices of Anthony-Ross on Denny Road.

They'd dropped everything and rushed down from Longview when Rob had called, only telling them to hurry, it was urgent.

Paula was waiting at the front desk, a blank expression on her face.

"Hi, Paula. The guys are expecting me," Byron practically gasped.

"Hello, Byron. They'll be just a moment."

"Is there something the matter?"

"I think this is a conversation you'd better have with them," she replied blankly, answering the phone for another Shared Secretarial client.

Byron glanced nervously at Nancy. What could this be? He'd known about the problems with the demonstration unit at the Wauna Mill, which had continued. But they were a team, and he was in this thing for the long haul. He had even rolled up his sleeves and helped out Bud and Clint, nights and weekends at Industrial Machine Shop, trying to make this thing work better. *Is that what this is about?*

Paula hung up the phone. "Byron, Tom and Rob will see you now." He and Nancy rose nervously. Something was definitely up. Making him wait in the lobby? Being summoned? Byron took his wife's hand and slowly headed down the hall, almost afraid to open the door to the tiny office.

"Everything okay, Tom?" Byron asked as they walked in.

"Well Byron, we have a little problem," Tom answered, his face giving away nothing. "Nancy, we wanted you here, too. I'm afraid you both need to hear this."

"What is it, Tom?," she demanded. "What's going on?"

"Why don't I let Rob tell you?"

"Byron, Nancy." Rob began somberly, "We do have a little problem. Well, I should say, *you* have the problem." He reached to the floor and pulled up a rectangular piece of poster board, 3 feet by 5 feet.

"Of getting this into your car and down to the bank."

He turned the huge cardboard around and broke into the biggest grin in Oregon that day. It was an Anthony-Ross check, made out to Byron and Nancy Goodspeed, for $25,360 - his share of the first commercial purchase of the Anthony Ross APC system.

I was there when the call had come in five days before, when Fletcher Smith called, confirming Temple East-Tex's purchase order for the Anthony-Ross Port Cleaning system for $340,000. You could hear the whoops, shouts, and high-fives three blocks away. When the deposit check for $91,000 arrived the next day, we whooped and hollered again. We'd waited 18 months for that check.

I got to be there for this moment too. This time, as Paula, Vic, and I stepped in to join Rob and Tom, Nancy and Byron, the laughter of a perfectly executed practical joke turned to a thoughtful moment of silence, and then joyful, grateful, and satisfied tears. For all of us, the dreams and genius of a quirky millwright and those of two young and inexperienced, tenaciously determined engineer-entrepreneurs had become reality.

After more than a year and a half, Anthony-Ross had their first sale. It was the breakthrough they'd worked for since Day One.

And none of us would ever be the same.

Chapter Eight
The Magic "E"

Tom Ross' eyes were bleary after a morning on the computer. He pushed back from his desk, happy for the reason to take at least a short walk down the hall; the mail had just arrived. He said hello to Paula, and casually flipped through the usual stack of bills, invoices and junk mail, and nearly missed one envelope from Crown-Zellerbach.

Tom stopped dead in his tracks. He knew what this was, and he knew that the future of the Anthony-Ross Company literally hinged on the enclosed document. He stepped back into his empty office, closed the door behind him, and sat back down.

"This is it," he thought to himself, as he held the envelope. In a few seconds time, he would have a very clear idea of whether his company was going to make it or not.

He took a deep breath, and opened the envelope.

The joy of that first sale lingered a few days, but it was soon replaced by the knowledge that one sale does not a company make. The Temple-East-Tex deal was a hugely important milestone to be sure, but there was always the possibility that this one sale would be their last. There was still a puzzle piece missing, and until they got it, Tom knew the company wasn't completely out of the woods.

Crown Zellerbach owned the mill in Wauna, Oregon. They had been sufficiently impressed, weeks before, with Rob and Tom's presentation to order a demonstration unit. But like the others, offered up little hope that they would actually purchase the Anthony-Ross APC system. Same old song: **too expensive, without a proof of savings**.

That very afternoon, Rob and Tom returned to the office and started an all-night brainstorming session. *How can we prove what we're selling?*

Tom had been working on creating a computer program that would clearly and irrefutably measure the boiler results, and demonstrate the savings that the Anthony-Ross system would deliver, in dollars and cents. Like their college days in the computer lab, he and Rob worked through the night to finish that program. By sunrise, they felt they had the best version possible, and a bulletproof plan. They drove back out to Wauna with "an offer the mill couldn't refuse:"

Pay us only on the basis of your savings.

It was very simple, and therein laid its genius. It was basically just a profit-sharing plan. Anthony-Ross maintained that with their APC operating on the boiler, the Wauna Mill's energy costs would drop, efficiency would rise, thereby giving them a new operating profit margin of $340,000, which was the purchase price Tom and Rob assigned the system. Essentially, it was no money out. If it failed to meet this number, the mill paid nothing beyond the installation cost. If it went beyond $340K, Anthony-Ross would be paid a percentage of the new profit margin.

How could they lose?

The mill agreed, and Tom and Rob installed the system. The guys had to purchase newer measuring equipment, convert Wauna's measuring system from analog to digital, and they had to perfect the actual computer program. It took several months, it cost Anthony-Ross a fair amount of time and money, and it wasn't all smooth sailing. You will recall, there was some drama, more than a few headaches, and some late night "adjustments" out at the mill.

Now, the results were in. It all came down to what was inside this envelope. It would be a blizzard of numbers, utterly meaningless to most of us, but not to the writer of the computer program and the installer of the unit to begin with. They were the same numbers being analyzed by the engineers out at Wauna, and numbers don't lie. Tom knew the whole story before he got to page two.

The Anthony-Ross system did not deliver $340,000 in savings to the mill.

It delivered $374,000. It wouldn't take an engineer to understand this curve of efficiency; a fourth grader could see it. The mill called before the afternoon was out, and... go figure... Anthony-Ross had their second sale, for that exact amount.

But they had much more than that. They had what they'd been searching for since they and Byron were granted the patent on the Automatic Port Cleaner; the most critical piece of that puzzle, the piece that would ultimately make or break this company...

"The Magic E" in the Anthony-Ross CEMO: **The Evidence**.

Now indeed, the company was finally and *truly* Off to the Races.

Chapter Nine
"Failure Is Not an Option"

He didn't know it, but Todd Hill had been waiting in the wings since Anthony-Ross moved from "Associates" to "Company." Todd, you may recall, was a fellow engineer, friend, and kindred spirit to Tom and Rob. He'd actually set up their first pitch meetings with the Flow-Meter.

Todd was still working for Bingham Willamette as a corporate engineer. It was a good job, if not the most satisfying in the world to a born hands-on guy. Still, he was the first of the guys to marry and start a family, and a good engineering job is a fine thing at that station in life. He was considering changing companies, taking an offer from Boeing, when Rob and Tom had him down for a celebratory reunion at their old pizza and pitchers hangout.

"I raise my mug, gentlemen," Todd began his toast. "To the Anthony-Ross Company and their first sale."

"Hear, hear," the guys clinked mugs in response.

"Sure took you long enough," Todd razzed, smiling.

"That's because we didn't have you working with us," Tom said, grabbing another slice of pizza. "We could have cut that time in half."

"That's true, Tom," Todd nodded sarcastically. "I am a Rain-maker, aren't I?"

"That's kinda the way we see it, Todd. So why don't you, then?" Rob zeroed in, serious as could be.

"Why don't I what?"

"Come to work with us," Tom finished the thought.

"I was kidding, guys."

"We weren't."

Todd was more than a good friend; he was also a Class-A engineer. He was organized, smart, had an accounting background, and already had four years working for a giant company as an engineer. This is a no-brainer, right?

Not so fast. Going to work with your friends in their fledgling start-up was a no-brainer four years ago, which for Todd was pre-wife, pre-mortgage, and pre-kids.

Let's broaden this story's focus from the two guys that started this company for a moment, and look at a man standing on the sidelines of the Anthony-Ross Company with a completely different set of circumstances. Let's return once more to the opening chapter, and the three fundamental traits of the entrepreneur: Passion, Spirit of Independence, and the Willingness to Take a Risk. That night in the pizza joint, only one of them was crystal clear in the case of Todd Hill.

Todd was, and remains to this day, passionate about his work as an engineer and a problem solver, but he had gone to work immediately out of college for a major corporation. Good, bad, or ugly, it was the only adult working condition he had known up to this point.

I certainly hope that my position on working for another has not been misconstrued. Aside from the inevitable corporate politics and loss of some degree of independence working for a big company brings, you really can't ignore the stress that is *removed* by a steady bi-monthly paycheck, medical and retirement benefits with the strong potential for growth in all three.

A newly-married guy in his first house with his first kid, with an offer to go to work for what many considered a dream company in the 80s and 90s - Boeing? Todd was independent spirited enough to be enticed by his friends' offer, but let's just call this offer exactly what it was: a serious roll of Todd Hill's life dice.

Todd would be a huge asset for Anthony-Ross, there was no doubt about it, but this was still a brand new and relatively inexperienced engineering sales firm. Sure, they had two deals and a ream of test data from Wauna, but that didn't exactly make them a blue-chip stock offering. They might offer him a competitive salary for a year, maybe two, but if the ship goes down, as start-ups are known to do now and again, would Todd have another ship to jump to? If that scenario did come to pass, how much impact would a couple years off the corporate scene with a failed start-up actually have on his career?

It's one thing to risk all that as a young engineer in a cracker box bachelor apartment with no other financial or life obligations, but Todd wasn't at this place in life anymore. All the rest of it aside, his life-partner, who counted on him holding up his end of their forever arrangement, was at home putting the baby to sleep. This decision was not his to make alone, nor should it have been.

The overwhelming majority of people are plenty passionate and have more than a healthy dose of independence in their spirit, but it's this last trait that tips the balance: willingness to take a risk. Some just can't. The price of failure is just too high to roll that life-dice. There is no shame in making that calculation, and letting a dream opportunity pass.

"Tell me what you're thinking," Tom sat back, looking at his friend.

"I'm thinking I need to talk this over with my wife."

I don't know all the dynamics of the discussion between Todd and his wife that weekend, or the week that followed. Maybe it was her belief in her husband and trust in the judgment that had so far put him on the fast-track to success, or maybe her own independent spirit and willingness to take a risk. She knew Todd could easily have spent a nice and comfortable career as a corporate guy, but that's not where his heart was. I think Todd was a tad surprised when she blessed this chance they would both be taking together.

He called Rob and Tom up at work the next Friday. He'd given his two–week notice at Bingham Willamette, and wouldn't be taking the Boeing job. He'd be coming to work with them.

The first order for Anthony-Ross essentially made the company $240,000 after they manufactured the system and paid Byron his commission. The next item on the agenda was to pay off all their debt, which was about $75,000. And that they did!

I doubt I need to linger on this point, especially at this moment in America's economic history, which was triggered largely by "debt," but it doesn't go without saying, so let's just say it again. Debt is a hindrance to a company, a nation, or an individual. Your parents taught you this. Painful experience with credit cards and other easy debt teaches us this. Most every religious text out there very accurately calls debt *slavery*.

I was particularly taken by this choice the partners made, with no prompting from me or their Board. They could easily have justified paying back little or none at all in this first sale, going ahead and expanding the operation. At the very least, they could have given themselves a nice bonus or a much-deserved break on a beach somewhere, after that bearish eighteen months of start-up time.

But they didn't do any of those. They paid back all their investors' loans, bumped their own salaries to something more realistic for 70-hour work-weeks, hired Todd Hill as a third engineer, and got back to work.

There was still a huge hole in the organization. The guys needed a secretary.

Now the term "secretary" has gotten short shrift in this era of high-flying managers and fast-track MBA-wielding executives. The fact of the matter is no matter your brilliance in sales, deal-making, engineering, or whatever your Fortune 500 CEMO may be, if you can't write a decent business letter and organize your operation, you'll be a ship lost at sea in no time, especially if your enterprise begins to succeed.

Tom and Rob had done a great job of juggling their responsibilities as engineers and salesmen with the full-time job of running a business and the very office itself. Paula Zimmerman had saved the day more than once, but Paula worked for someone else full-time. Meanwhile, Rob and Tom were both drowning in detail. They needed someone who could jump in with little or no training and handle that detail.

Lue Paddock fit that bill to a tee, and then some.

Lue had been an executive secretary for more than twenty years, and had considered retiring when the company she'd been with most of that time was sold. Instead, she signed on to another corporation, and it had been a personal and professional disaster.

"No morals, no ethics, people treating each other awfully," she recalls that time leading up to the fateful day she answered Tom and Rob's ad in the paper. "I was so discouraged by this experience that I never wanted to work for anyone ever again."

And she didn't really have to. Still, Lue just wasn't the sort to sit back and take it easy, and besides, she was too young to retire anyway. Her resume spoke for itself. She was actually way over-qualified both for the position and the salary Anthony-Ross was offering, but-

"I knew the instant I walked in that office and met these two, I was taking this job whether they offered it or not," she laughs. "Now that I've been with Anthony-Ross so long, it makes perfect sense that all these 'miracles' kept happening to these guys and their company."

She started right away, and they became "her boys." Years working at the highest corporate levels brought a wisdom and operating efficiency that three 20-something engineers could never muster. More importantly, her love for this company and the qualities and values set forth by its founding partners made her much more than just an employee. From Day One, she was an integral and necessary part of the Anthony-Ross Team. She stayed with the company more than twenty years.

The company was moving and growing, but the challenges had only just begun.

Rob's voice on the phone from Orange, Texas a few weeks later was one of discouragement, bordering on despair. "Tom, this thing's come loose again."

"Oh you gotta be kidding me," Tom answered groggily. This late-night call brought the same sense of foreboding as the one he'd taken a couple weeks ago from the Crown Zellerbach Mill up in Wauna. "What time is it there?"

"Two-thirty. Buddy, this situation has passed the critical stage. If we don't get this thing working right, they'll want their money back."

"Okay, Rob. I'm heading to the office. Call me in a half-hour."

The elation of the new deal with Temple-East Tex was quickly replaced by the frustration of an installation nightmare. Nearly forty individual port cleaners were manufactured by Anthony-Ross with Industrial Machine, and shipped to Texas. Tom and Rob had both installed them, and both partners had been back at least three times fixing subsequent problems.

The port sizes were not all uniform; some of the cleaning units didn't match up to their ports. Parts were indeed coming loose. The tips of the cleaners themselves were fouling and failing too quickly. Even the windows were cracking.

To put it mildly, the millwrights, boiler operators, and Mill Manager were not pleased. Those walks into the mill were every bit as Dead Man Walking for Rob as Tom's had been that night up at Wauna, which brings us back to the prologue scene for this first Book. The picture was still very similar for Tom up at the Crown Zellerbach Mill. They didn't just slap these babies on the boiler, collect a check, and go home. This was a new system, and there were bugs a-plenty yet to work out. The newest Anthony-Ross employee, Todd Hill who'd been assigned to oversee at the Weyerhaeuser Mill in Kamloops, Canada, was working through the same sorts of bugs, and the folks there weren't happy about it, either.

The idea was sound. The design was great. The units were manufactured on time and on-budget, and installed carefully and with maniacal attention to detail by the obviously very principled engineer-founders of this company who'd given every working day of their lives for two years to these units...

AND THEY WEREN'T WORKING!

This wasn't just a speed-bump or a growing pain for the now up and operating engineering firm. With their first three units in the field, and all three very problematic, in a business where word travels at the speed of light, the Anthony-Ross Company was suddenly in more peril than they were with no sales. In truth, they were on the brink of complete and total failure.

Tom and Rob, and now Todd, were always off the charts as far as their optimism, passion, work ethic, integrity, and tenacity were concerned. The company had ridden through a couple of very, very tough years, but nothing had been even remotely close to this; the edge of disaster, the breaking point, the collapse.

Make no mistake about it, if these three units failed - and at that moment they were indeed failing - this game was over. There would not be a comeback. Let's just say that if that fate became real, they wouldn't be the prime candidates in an ever-growing crop of engineers looking for jobs out there.

Unbelievably, with three sales, no company debt, and a terrific team being put together, this was their darkest moment yet.

Psychologists tell us that one of the two greatest human fears is that of failure. Nobody likes to fail; nobody sets out to fail. Here's the most cruel truth of all: sometimes great ideas and great people fail, and there is no clear reason for why they do!

It would be absurd to write a book about success and not visit this powerful counter-force. Let's just say it like it is. More entrepreneurial enterprises fail than succeed. There's no way to sugarcoat that. That's real, that's life. When we play a game, there will be a winner and a loser. Same with any contest, whether it's a round of golf, a peach cobbler at a county fair, or a national election.

A business is no exception.

I mean, look. It's not fair, is it? Look at these guys - the Poster Boys for the 12 Steps of Character, for heavens sake! Eagle scouts aspire to be Tom, Rob, and now Todd's equal as far as their personal and professional code of ethics goes. They have dedicated their young lives to the hard work of studying engineering, licensing an industry-changing invention, and taking care of that inventor far better than they had to. They have sacrificed everything to build their small business and literally change lives with their integrity and how they treat people.

Is it fair that these guys could actually fail?

That's the wrong question. It has no answer, so it is a waste of time even asking it. So why ask it at all? Because it's human nature. We **all** do it.

I've been at this game sixty years, folks, and I'm here to tell you that there is absolutely no guarantee in this world of success at anything. Guarantees don't exist. I'll say again what I said when we watched Tom walk across that mill ground at the beginning of our time together. If you launch any venture of any size and scope, you will one day have a moment like this. It may not be as intense, the stakes may not be as high, but the only guarantee the Entrepreneur's

Way is offering you is this one. If you get in this game, you will have to face one of our worst fears… the fear of failure.

The only question worth asking, then, is what will you do at that moment?

There is a line from an old movie, reminds my co-author, which goes something like this. When things are at their worst, human beings are at their best. Well, after a rip-roaring breakthrough, things were now pretty much at their worst for the Anthony-Ross Company. One more month of this, and the doors would close. It was time for these guys to rise to the occasion, and be at their very best.

So here's what Tom, Rob and Todd did. They sat down together and went over their options:

Hire this problem out to a consultant

Keep beating their heads against the wall, and buying time with the Mills till they figured it out

Throw in the towel

Well, they didn't have the time or, quite honestly, the resources to hire out a consultant. As for the second option, they could just work harder, but they were at their wits end. When they fixed one thing, another would break. If there was a Killer App, it was escaping them.

Throw in the towel, then?

Tom remembers a quiet moment of hesitation, with the three of them going over these options around the drafting table at midnight - the same table they'd been poring over since that morning, with no solution. They were all thinking the exact same thing. It may not be up to them any longer. Like the Titanic, this thing felt like it was going to sink, and there wasn't a thing they could do about it.

In an instant, the moment passed. These guys had faced despair before. They weren't going to let this beat them. They just plain refused to quit.

"We're going to solve this," Tom solemnly declared at the darkest midnight any of them would ever remember. "But we're not going to do it alone. Let's go home, and get some sleep. Tomorrow morning, it's all hands on deck."

It was their *Apollo 13* Moment. If you remember that wonderful movie, based on the very true story of a spaceship essentially dead in space, you remember a roomful of engineers using everything from a vacuum cleaner hose to paper clips, working round the clock 'til they figured out how to rig up a solution for Jim Lovell and his crew to get home. Maybe you remember the wonderful words spoken as they commenced:

"FAILURE IS NOT AN OPTION."

For the next six weeks, Byron and the Industrial Machine guys, Bud and Clint, were in the room for what seemed 24/7 days with Tom, Rob, and Todd. They drew, they re-drew, they argued. They flew back and forth, tinkering, re-machining, and working on-site with the engineers and millwrights at all three of the installations. It wasn't a big happy club at the beginning but, by the end, Anthony-Ross wasn't just some contracted engineering firm. They and Byron and Bud and Clint and the mill workers were all brothers in arms in the foxhole together.

I want to apologize to my engineering readers for the lack of micro-detail in the Big Breakthrough - the calm and rational "That's it" moment - which did indeed come in this *Apollo 13* time, but the authors are not engineers. The nuts and bolts particulars of a complete re-design and re-installation of the APC system are out of our liberal arts-educated grasp, but the lesson here goes far beyond engineering.

The point is that **it worked**. Different and fresh points of view, the freedom to speak even in disagreement, the line in the sand decision that not only would there be no towel thrown in, they would die on this hill before giving up...

It was at this moment that Anthony-Ross completed its journey, first from "Associates" to "Company," and then to the most valuable place any organization or venture can hope to get. And it is this place that every organization aspires to reach, when we transcend simple commerce and work together with our employees, our consultants, even our customers in a dogged fight to overcome an obstacle - to win a hard-fought game *together*.

The Anthony-Ross Company and everyone in business with them now, were a *Team*.

Chapter Ten
Growing Pains

It was a quantum leap. No, it wasn't the three or four now-successful installations, or the suddenly improved cash flow, or even the further building of the company with project engineers and support staff. The quantum leap for the Anthony-Ross Company stemmed from their biggest hindrance: the ability to measure their results.

From the beginning, no one ever doubted Rob and Tom when they boldly stated that the APC would be an improvement to their boiler systems. Likewise, no one doubted that it would save them money. The question was, *how much* and how long would it take for their investment of up to a half-million dollars to be recouped in those savings?

They could not answer the question, not with any certainty anyway. Now, three units were operating nicely and collecting reams of data for that computer of theirs to process. The results were even better than they'd hoped. The numbers proved their original claim with authority. This was the evidence their CEMO was missing. Now that they had it, this little company was moving at full speed by 1985.

But by no means were the challenges behind them.

The mental hurdle now facing Rob and Tom was the fear of growing. It's understandable, of course, looking back at what they fondly recall as their "Days of Ramen Noodles," that they would be hesitant to start expanding and hiring other people. They were certainly competent at pretty much every area of their operation at this point. Tom was married now, though Rob was getting serious about a girl, and they were used to working tirelessly, being in the loop on each decision made. Todd, the one married guy, seemed to fill any engineering gap they had right now, as well as running this company. Lue Paddock was more than capable of handling any administrative issue that came their way. Why grow, when the safe course would just be to keep chugging along as a little engineering company.

They might very well have, if that data they had needed for so long hadn't started leaking out in a fairly small industry to begin with. The phones weren't silent anymore. They didn't have to explain who they were now. The mills were coming to them. Even Weyerhaeuser, with whom they'd had a little speed-bump at the very beginning, had completed their great circle in buying the system for their mill at Kamloops. That was important because it signaled to the paper industry that the leader of that industry was in business with Anthony-Ross.

The decision was being made for them. They couldn't just chug along as a little engineering company. They had to commit to grow.

Why would this be a problem? Wasn't this what they'd always dreamed and envisioned for their company since the day Rob introduced Tom to Byron, and his first-generation port cleaner? Of course it was. Then the reality of starting and running a company descended on them like the proverbial ton of bricks.

It is pretty much a universal truth: these things never go as fast and easy as you think they will. Failure's Sword of Damocles always looms over the start-up. After nearly two years of no sales and then three nightmare installations where their company stood at the brink of disaster, these still-optimistic guys couldn't be blamed for wondering when "the other shoe might drop." Something had to go wrong, a competitor could knock them right off the block, a brand new technology could come along and make this system obsolete, who knew what the future might hold.

It was one thing for the two of them to go through the "Days of Ramen Noodles" together as unmarried roommates and partners. It was quite another to bring in others, commit to their salaries and profit-sharing and benefits, with that memory so close.

Is this the Fear of Success then? No. It's the biggest fear of them all, folks, and the one we all share. It's the Fear of the Unknown.

All Tom and Rob had known up to this point was difficulty, struggle, and, yes, a healthy dose of failure. Now suddenly, they were right where they always wanted to be, and having a hard time going to the next level.

That next level is the slightly uncomfortable process of trusting and letting go.

Oh how I would love to tell you that in so doing, all their problems disappeared and they sailed into the happy sunset of a "4 Hour Workweek" and a life brimming over with continued success, comfort, and riches. I bet they would have loved that, too.

Too bad it didn't work out that way.

The guys decided that maybe they were just too close to the company to really have an objective Big Picture view of it all. I seconded that conclusion as their advisor. I believe we discussed a possible "coming out of retirement" for me to come on board as an operations manager or some similar function, and I considered it. I even had an office in the same building with them now. But quite honestly, I thought I was too close to it all, too. Besides, I'd been "retired" for precisely a year in 1986, after having worked pretty much non-stop since 1952. My Fear of the Unknown was long gone as far as retirement went. My wife and I were having a ball traveling, playing tennis and golf, and visiting our other kids. I loved my role as Board Member and Advisor, and wasn't hungry to expand it.

It didn't take long for Anthony-Ross to find a very competent manager to come in, learn the operation, and generally take much of the administrative load off the shoulders of Rob, Tom, and Todd. Once they all got used to the idea of a lot more free time to return to their first professional love—pure engineering—not to mention more of a personal life after 6:00 at night and on weekends, the guys kind of liked it.

Lasted about two months.

He was a fine man, a solid professional, and an accomplished manager and strategic thinker. The problem was his strategic direction did not at all agree with theirs. He wanted to branch Anthony-Ross out into manufacturing. They were practically doing it already with their constant upgrading and spare parts fabricating with the guys at Industrial Machine. Just make it official, phase them out, and double the operations here overnight, was his thinking.

Tom put his foot down immediately. No way. Bud and Clint at Industrial Machine shop in Kelso had been too loyal. They were there at the beginning, and Tom and Rob both felt they owed the success of this company to them as much as anyone. The manager didn't see it that way. He and Anthony-Ross parted on friendly terms. So much for the guys letting go.

This running question for an entrepreneur is always close at hand: When and how much to "let go." The only real answer to that question is "it depends." There are a myriad of factors, really, but the single most important one is that of the Entrepreneur's Vision, and his or her comfort with changing or at least augmenting that vision, not to mention putting that change in the hands of someone else. There is a fine line running between trust, loyalty to a vision, and just plain fear of the unknown. Also, there's always the very stubborn human refusal to alter a course.

They probably would have made more money had they gone with this new strategy of not only designing and installing, but adding the manufacture of the product, increasing their workload, liability, and stress level. The way Tom saw it, they were maxed on all three. Industrial Machine couldn't have done a better job of making that decision easy. They were successful because of them.

"I don't know, maybe we were too worried and paranoid about our reputation. We were ever aware that one false step, a poor installation, or unhappy customer would be poison to us," Tom tells me now. "This was our mindset *without* adding in the manufacturing! Right or wrong, we were motivated by fear. On the other hand, fear is a powerful motivator."

The truth was that Rob and Tom's original vision of a small development and sales firm remained. They were willing to augment it a tad by growing, but not by changing direction into a process they didn't know or truly understand.

They stuck with what they knew. Whether fear of the unknown was the determining factor or not, it was the right call.

But a darker challenge was coming up fast.

Up to this point, every hiring decision was made after an exhaustive process of getting to know the individual personally as well as professionally. From the secretaries to the engineers, it was critical to Tom and Rob that the operating philosophy of Anthony-Ross remained intact: this company was a *Team*. The management would not be the traditional Boss-Employee approach, with all its attendant baggage. From the founding partners on down, the code of conduct demanded was one of mutual respect, regardless of job title.

It was obvious within days that their newly-hired Sales Manager did not share this philosophy. Oh, he'd interviewed just fine, and his resume spoke for itself. He had good references and was obviously successful at sales. Suddenly, Anthony-Ross was moving at warp speed. Inquiries were rolling in faster than they could write them down. They needed somebody right now. The usual exhaustive procedure of vetting and getting to know the new-hire was put aside. *The guy fits the bill; let's hire him!*

And therein lay the first mistake.

He hadn't been there a week before the first snide comment toward a "subordinate" flew. There were questions about his honesty. His treatment of others began to poison what had been a very relaxed and happy team atmosphere at work. When he verbally abused one of the night-cleaning staff, Tom had enough. He confronted the man and, in no uncertain terms, let him know that this conduct would not be tolerated here. This was his one and only warning.

"I should have fired him on the spot," Tom recalls the incident now. "He was a terrible fit to our Team. And the longer he stayed, the worse it got."

So why didn't fire him on the spot? With the benefit of time, it's easy to see that this man simply did not belong here, and he needed to go. The answer is simple; it isn't easy to fire someone. It's human nature is to put off difficult decisions, and certainly confrontations, and hope that bad situations will resolve themselves. The problem is that they usually don't.

The second and more serious mistake here was indecision. The reasons were many, varied, and logical, but the bottom line is that the guys put off the inevitable. Tom was only in his mid-twenties. This was Anthony-Ross' first serious Human Resources challenge. He can be forgiven the hesitation, but he is right? Should he or Rob have fired this guy on the spot.

STEP #10. I MAKE DECISIONS

Please don't misunderstand. I am not advocating the Terminator approach to management - one mistake and you're on the street. I am merely stating the obvious. Remember what your Mom told you as a child. "One bad apple will spoil the whole bunch." That's absolutely true. It didn't get better with this man; it got worse. His dishonesty, attitude, and treatment of others began eating away at the Team morale in this company. In time, he could have literally sunk the Anthony-Ross ship. It finally fell to Todd when he took the helm a few years later to fire him.

The lesson here is simple. We don't want to make snap decisions in this life, but putting off a decision almost never works, especially when it's as obvious as this situation. Firing someone is difficult and unpleasant, and should be done only after every other avenue is exhausted. However, in the end, just like in sports, the Team has to come first.

Ironically, soon after his firing, the man tried to set up his own rival company using the technology and practices he'd learned at Anthony-Ross. It failed.

And the Anthony-Ross growing pains continued.

The guys got pretty excited about an international presence when a Swedish company came to call, wanting to enter into a European licensing agreement. After a couple of fun but ultimately mystifying trips to Stockholm and the signing of a formal agreement, complete radio silence settled in. It didn't take long for them to figure out what had happened. The company was essentially taking advantage of the distance between them, and ripping the little company off by copying their system, manufacturing and selling the units themselves in Scandinavia, with of course no knowledge and certainly no license fee or royalty for Anthony-Ross. The only way Rob and Tom were made even aware of the situation was that the systems weren't working properly, when they worked at all. They, of course, scrambled to terminate their agreement, and made sure every single mill there knew what had transpired.

This bad news actually turned out to be great news. This awful turn of events made it clear to all the Scandinavian paper companies that the competitive advantage of the Anthony-Ross APC wasn't the unit itself. The competitive advantage was **them**!

Well, any successful operation is going to get noticed eventually. Sometimes that's good, sometimes that's not so good. For nearly three years, Anthony-Ross was on an uninterrupted upward trajectory. Yes, of course there were growing pains. That's just part of this process. All that time, though, they were the only game in town or, more accurately as you just saw, the only serious Automatic Port Cleaning game *in the world*.

They and their unit got better every single job, and they were now the *de facto* industry leader in cleaning industrial boilers. They would design the unit, and outsource but supervise the manufacture to the now substantially expanded Industrial Machine shop in Longview. Note: Bud and Clint and their son in law Rocky named their new production wing after Anthony-Ross, and Byron was now retired from Weyco, and there every day. Anthony-Ross had even sprouted a huge, but originally unforeseen business in the spare parts realm. This was a success story for all the world to see.

...including a company that decided they could knock Anthony-Ross off that pedestal.

Diamond Power was an Industrial Machine manufacturer that also served the pulp paper industry. The rapid deployment of the Anthony-Ross Company's APC did not escape their attention, and their R&D department set out to make their own. It was legal. Anthony-Ross had a patent on Byron's design, but not on the concept of a port cleaner. They were a bigger company, had resources and relationships and, sure enough, got their first sale to one of Anthony-Ross' prospective customers—*at a hundred thousand dollars less*! Anthony-Ross lost the sale.

I think to describe this event as the company's Pearl Harbor might be a tad over the top, but it was a show-stopper, and in the entire history of the company, the only heated disagreement we ever had.

Think of it. After three years of being the only ones even in this business, and getting comfortable with that thought and making plans and projections on that thought, a competitor suddenly comes from out of nowhere and sells a unit for about a third less than your unit price. Once the shock wore off, the discussion had to turn to our response. There were only two possible responses: ignore it and keep right on doing what we'd been doing at the same price we'd been doing it, or keep on doing it and lower that price to stay competitive.

Rob and Vic chose lowering the price. This is natural. They were sales guys. They were already dreading the inevitable push-back that the mills would hit them with: why would we go with you when we can pay a hundred grand less for the same result?

Tom came at it from the cold reality of the numbers. Anthony-Ross could not possibly match that price and remain profitable. It was that simple. It would wipe out the future of the company.

This was not a casual disagreement. It struck at the core of the company's future. A mistake in either direction could spell the end. They were split right down the middle on this one. They needed a tiebreaker.

In the entire time I'd been with Anthony-Ross, even in the days when Rob and Tom were living in our basement, I went out of my way to never be seen playing favorites with my son. Many times, when he and Rob would have a disagreement in company matters, I'd side with Rob if the arguments were close enough together. If you ask Tom, he'll reply jokingly, I would side *against my son*.

But this was no joke, and these arguments were not close together. They were polar opposites in theory and in practice, and I didn't hesitate at all in coming to a conclusion, regardless of the appearance to Rob or Tom. This was not about the appearance of objectivity; this was about the company.

Don't lower your price, guys.

It's not rocket science. It doesn't take an MBA or 30 years running companies to come to that conclusion. First off, Tom was right about the numbers. They wouldn't make it in the long run, who knows, maybe even the short run. If they cut their price to match Diamond Power's, they'd have to cut costs dramatically. That always leads to quality control problems in technology. They were operating at about a 5:1 profit/cost ratio. They just couldn't dip much below that and keep their competitive edge.

More importantly, it was the philosophy of being proactive or *re-active*. It sends a signal to all, and that signal is not one of confidence and faith in your approach, your product, or its pricing. Put another way, a kneejerk reaction would not signal leadership and comfort in leadership.

We held the price. We went about our business, waiting and trying not to worry or even wonder about the fallout from Diamond Power's design and installation of an automatic port cleaner at $100,000 less than ours.

One year later, we got our answer. Their customer called. The Diamond Power port cleaner system didn't work. Would Anthony-Ross come out and give them a bid on a replacement system?

"We'd be delighted," was Tom and Rob's answer.

Chapter Eleven
When It's Time

"Earth to Rob...?"

Tom chuckled at his partner who was clearly preoccupied, staring off into space. It was nearly nine o'clock on a rainy night in late 1988. Todd, Lue, and the rest of the Anthony-Ross staff had gone home hours ago. It was just Tom and Rob at their desks, the last to leave tonight. Just like the old days.

"You've been looking out the window for the last half hour, man. Everything okay?" Tom continued.

"Yeah, fine. Fine." Rob shuffled papers on his desk, looking for something to do, it seemed. He didn't find it.

Tom pushed away from his computer screen. "What's on your mind, pard?"

Rob took a deep breath. "You know how you and Vic always joke that you guys are my warm-up congregation?"

Tom smiled. It was true. Rob loved talking about religion as much or more as he did talking about the company. Nobody ever seemed to mind, though. It wasn't proselytizing; it was just a guy passionate about God. The guy had a gift. He was known to start some discussions at morning coffee that continued all day long while they worked.

"I've been thinking a lot about that lately. And maybe even..." Rob hesitated, "Exploring the next steps?"

Tom smiled. "I've been wondering when this would come up."

Five years had positively flown by. After seeming to stand still for those agonizing first eighteen months, the company took off at warp speed the minute they framed that first purchase order and put it on the wall. Anthony-Ross was going full tilt now, nearly $7 million in annual sales, selling and installing units all over the country, and doing a brisk business in spare parts. Twelve employees now, they were looking to hire some more engineers, maybe one more salesperson. Bud and Clint up at Industrial Machine had other customers, of course, but it was the constant flow of Anthony-Ross production orders that built a whole new machine shop for them.

Todd Hill turned out to be the missing piece the company puzzle had needed from the beginning. His skills as an engineer, administrator, and people guy complemented Tom and Rob's skills perfectly. The company wasn't exactly running itself, but the Sword of Damocles days were gone now. Times were good, and very, very busy.

Still, they were kids when they started, but they weren't kids anymore. A lot of life had happened to the founding partners of the Anthony-Ross Company since leaving college and starting out on their Entrepreneur's Way.

Tom married Francie McGrannahan in 1984, her senior year in college. They started a family right away, and had two kids already in 1988. She'd been patient with his borderline workaholic ways, but he'd made an agreement with her that it wouldn't always be twelve-plus hour work days, six and seven days a week. Rob was married now too. He'd met Laurie Mishler at a wedding in 1985. They tied the knot the next year, and were also ready to start a family.

Suddenly Anthony-Ross wasn't the singular, oft-times *maniacal*, focus of their lives, as most start-ups become in their formative years for their founders. Bigger, more important questions than business were being asked in the quiet of both their hearts as each hit the milestone age of thirty.

"You know I've been kinda into my faith for a while." Rob continued.

"Certainly since I've known you," Tom nodded.

"I've been thinking a lot about the Big Picture, you know. I'm not saying when, but I think maybe I'd like to look more seriously at… you know, the possibility of…"

"Becoming a minister?" Tom finished for him, laughing. "Gee, Rob, *this just in!*"

"So, you knew?"

"Well of course I knew. How could I not know? And buddy, you *should.*"

Rob exhaled in relief. He'd been dreading this conversation for weeks. He should have known better. "Laurie and I have been talking this out for a while now. I wasn't sure before, but now, I really believe I'm being called, Tom."

"Rob, I think it's great. I think you're gonna be a terrific preacher. And I think you should get on it now, before you guys start having kids."

"What do I do about the company, then?" Rob asked quietly.

"The question is what do **we** do about the company?' Tom smiled at Rob's puzzled expression. "Francie and I have been talking, too. I'm never home, and I want to be. My kids aren't gonna be this age forever. The company is solid, and we've got orders for the next three years. I think Todd would like a shot at running the place himself. Lord knows he could do it."

"Yeah, he could."

"I don't know, Rob. Maybe it's time."

Rob had quietly been looking into seminaries. Tom had actually started another business on the side, Precision Testing, Inc. He really loved the process of start-up, and was surprised to find out how much he loved working out of the house. He too was looking at going back to school to get better on his first technological love, electronics.

There had been offers to buy the company, but none that felt remotely worth the time and sweat they both had put into this venture. They loved what they were doing and they loved the people they were doing it with. If the offer wasn't great, and they weren't completely comfortable with the buyers, they just weren't going to sell. It was that simple.

But things were changing, clearly.

Theirs were the last two cars in the parking lot. Rob and Tom walked out together wordlessly, thinking the same thing; they had done what they had set out to do. Neither had set a goal past getting their company up and running, but that's exactly where they were right now, and they'd been there for a while. Just as they had reached the decision to launch the Anthony-Ross Company together, they reached this milestone decision together as well.

Tom and Rob were ready to move on.

It's a big deal when the founders of a company sell it, with the intention of leaving right away. Rob and Tom told the Board of their decision at the beginning of 1989, and we instigated the process of (very) quietly letting the investment community know that the company was for sale. The guys were not secretive by nature, but it was all the Board's experience that word of this getting out would not only cause instability in the company, it could completely derail the sale. Their biggest concern was for the continued health and longevity of Anthony-Ross.

Fortunately, there was Todd Hill. Rob and Tom had told him of their decision. He was a bit taken aback, but also saw a great opportunity to take the helm of the company, and he was the perfect guy to do it. Todd had the same entrepreneurial spirit in the first place. He also endorsed their management style, with respect for the individual taking first priority. He would take care of Byron, and ensure that the reputation of the company continued. Now, he would not only be able to take some true equity in the company, he could take the wheel himself in piloting it into the future.

By the way, he did all of the above, and then some. For seventeen years, the company positively flourished under his leadership.

Once the decision was made, it all happened fast.

The first company that came to call waved cash, and that was about where the interest ended for Tom and Rob. Discussions about management philosophies and teamwork didn't seem to mean quite as much to these guys as bottom lines, assets, and P/E statements. Tom and Rob were not at all assured that the Anthony-Ross employees would be extended the same creative and professional freedom and basic respect the company was founded on, much less their continued sharing in the company's profits. The buyers were vague with their plans. For all Tom and Rob could tell, they might install their own management team and show the Anthony-Ross team the door, or maybe even flip the company.

Whatever it was, it just didn't feel right. They turned the first offer down.

Bergeman, a German company was next, and they came armed with plenty of knowledge about Anthony-Ross, its core business, and the management philosophy and style of its founders. Bergeman manufactured air systems for the paper industry in Europe, and was looking to penetrate the North America market. They were a reputable company and very strong financially. They studied the Anthony-Ross operation carefully, were sufficiently impressed with the team in place, and had no intention of replacing them. If it wasn't broke, why fix it? They even put it in writing.

This one felt right.

Selling a company, like selling a port cleaner or your house even, is a balancing act. Large or small, sales ultimately come down to reading the buyer, understanding what that buyer wants, and not dragging things out so long that the buyer's enthusiasm fades away. The ultimate goal is for the seller to get the price he desires, and the buyer to feel like he got a great deal. That's the textbook Win/ Win. Now Tom and Rob needed to figure out a number that would produce just that.

I had one piece of advice for the guys: *Don't do this alone.*

One of my friends, Ashton Marcus ("Mark") had recently retired as vice president of Ohmart Industries, and had negotiated the buying and selling of several companies in the course of his career. He was happy to jump back in the game and help Tom and Rob through the negotiation process. My fellow board member Cliff Carlsen arranged for one of his colleagues to act as the Anthony-Ross attorney.

Bergeman was a large, well-established outfit. They had clearly done plenty of due diligence. They knew this market, and they knew the Anthony-Ross Company. They were making no secret of the fact that they wanted to buy them outright. All Tom and Rob could do was wait for their offer, and hope for a good price. Right now, this big German company was in the driver's seat.

Or were they?

"Make a brochure," was Mark's first piece of guiding advice.

"Make a brochure?" the guys asked, incredulously. "We have one."

"Not for this, you don't," Mark smiled. "You have a nice sales piece to get customers to buy your product. These guys are buying a lot more than a port cleaner, they're buying your company."

This was a huge piece of advice, and as foundational to sales as establishing rapport. It would certainly be understandable for Tom and Rob to take an easier road, and simply let the success of their company speak for itself. Anthony-Ross had become a force in this market, and surely had a "blue book value" no different than a car or a house. But Mark's experience in this game taught them a very important lesson. If you turn over all the control in a negotiation to the other side, you're going to leave money on the table.

So the guys produced a wonderful little "brochure" that not only detailed the company's product line, strong financials, customers and leading edge position in the market, it emphasized the Team that made up the success of the Anthony-Ross Company. Tom and Rob focused most of the attention, not on themselves, but on the *others*: the engineers, the sales team, Todd Hill as the obvious choice to take over the helm as Chief Executive. This wasn't just modesty; it was the truth, and it was *smart*. It was a signal that they knew their company was at the top of its game, poised for an even bigger leap in market share and profitability. They presented the brochure to the buyer without stipulating a price.

Six weeks later, The Day arrived. The Bergeman Team of executives and attorneys arrived in Portland, and sat down with the Anthony-Ross Team—Tom, Rob, Mark, and an attorney at the Anthony-Ross offices. The meet-and-greet chat gave way to a couple hours of general and friendly discussions on the industry, management philosophies, the market, etc. Then, honoring the ancient tradition of all negotiations, a brief pause signaled it was time to get down to business.

"Gentlemen," the Bergeman attorney began, "We all know why we're here. I believe the moment has arrived for you to tell us your asking price for the Anthony-Ross Company."

Tom and Rob were prepared for this opening move, and remained wordless. It was Mark who replied. "With all due respect, gentlemen, we defer to Bergeman's obvious position in this industry, and your view of our company's value to your operation. We would like you to make an offer, rather than for us to quote a price."

Pause.

It was a wonderful movie moment. The older, more established company sitting across the table from this little upstart start-up, run by two guys who were not even thirty. The old established guys had to concede Round One to Anthony-Ross.

"Yes, well," answered the lead negotiator for Bergeman after a moment, "We would like to adjourn for a few moments to discuss this."

"Absolutely," answered Mark.

Now I do not believe for a moment that the Bergeman Team flew all the way in from Germany just to hear Tom and Rob's asking price. They had a very good idea of what this company was worth, and what they were willing to pay. Like any good negotiator, they were just figuring out the guys on the other side of the table, and looking for one of two upper-hand making possibilities: a) the guys might be underselling, or b) they had no idea what their company was really worth.

Neither was the case, and Mark wasn't about to give anyone that easy of an opening.

"We believe your company is worth six million dollars," the Bergeman negotiator announced, after they'd returned an hour later.

Tom and Rob stared wordlessly back at them, as instructed. Poker faced. No response or expression while Mark nodded blankly, shuffling papers. They made darn sure they didn't look at each other...

Because the offer was higher than they'd expected. Tom and Rob felt they could get $5 million for their company. Of course, in their own estimations, they thought Anthony-Ross was worth much more, they were simply estimating on the conservative side. And they'd also just grown accustomed to being bargained downward. That's just business.

Now here was this multi-national concern offering them a million more - surely Mark was just going through the motions here...

He wasn't. "You of course know that the projections show Anthony-Ross making $2.2 million in the third year alone," Mark finally responded. "Six million seems a little short."

Not a word from the other side. Tom remembers his heart leaping into his throat, but Mark never blinked. *We're up a million, take the six, Mark!,* he and Rob must have been thinking. But Mark hadn't done this for thirty years and not learned a thing or two.

"If you'll excuse us this time, we'll have to discuss this. We'll come back shortly with a response."

They were well out of sight and earshot when Tom and Rob broke into hysterical laughter, high-fives and fist-pumps. Mark smiled, and hustled them into Tom's office.

"Mark, that's awesome! Great job, man!" The boys congratulated their negotiator, fully expecting they'd go back in and sign that deal.

Nope.

Mark shook his head. "There's still some left. That's not their best offer. We're gonna counter."

"I don't know, Mark," Tom glanced nervously at Rob. "This is a pretty good price. Aren't we taking a chance they might back away?"

"They won't back away. They might not accept our counter, but they're not going anywhere."

"Are you sure, Mark?" asked Rob.

"I'm sure, Rob."

The two founding partners of the Anthony-Ross Company glanced at each other nervously, taking a deep breath. This was miles from their comfort zone, and the last thing they wanted was to blow this sale. But this was a game Mark knew very well. If the guys had learned anything, it was to listen to people who knew more than them.

"Okay, Mark," Rob and Tom nodded. "Let's counter."

"We believe Anthony-Ross is worth seven million, gentlemen," Mark answered once the meeting reconvened.

Stone-cold silence. Seemed to last forever. There was a grim look on the Bergeman faces.

"We have studied this very carefully," the Bergeman negotiator stated in his very precise European manner. "We believe we have offered you a fair price based on your financials."

This was the poker moment. Mark did not respond, his instinct and experience told him to wait for an opening.

"Besides," the Bergeman man continued suddenly, "We have no way of knowing that the projections you made will actually come to pass."

That was the opening, and Tom and Rob had to fight not to smile at a master negotiator at work.

Mark nodded thoughtfully, shuffled his papers some more, and finally answered. "Fair enough. What if we make the extra million contingent on the company's hitting those numbers? If they do, the price is seven million. If they don't, it's six."

"I knew by their faces he had 'em," remembers Tom now. "They liked the sound of a contingency. It was like an insurance policy."

After a third recess, the Bergeman guys shook on the deal. They accepted the counter-offer of $7 million, with that contingency. They agreed also to keep Todd Hill on as president, as well as the employees' benefits package, and the operating policies and philosophies of the Anthony-Ross Company intact. Their company values would not be swallowed up in a large corporate culture.

Now came the hard part. It was time to tell the Team.

The news of the sale was a surprise to all, except Todd, whom they'd told early on. They couldn't have done it any other way, honestly. There was so much emotion wrapped up in both the company and these two young men, and that's understandable. These people weren't just a company. Rob, Tom, Todd, Paula, Lue, Vic, Byron, Nancy, Bud, Clint, and a dozen others working here didn't see themselves as employees and employers. *They were family.*

When the news was announced, it was greeted with a mixture of emotions to say the least. Joy for "the boys" who'd just grabbed the brass ring of entrepreneurship, relief that each of them still had a job, along with the reassurance that all their benefits would continue. More than anything, there was the undeniable misty, bittersweet realization that this little dream ride was over.

There literally wasn't a dry eye in the place when Tom and Rob broke the news.

Oh, the Anthony-Ross Company is not only still a viable company, twenty years after this moment, it remains the industry leader. Forty people call it their company now. Todd steered them brilliantly for seventeen years as president, the company's best days were actually ahead of them.

But none of that was real the day Tom and Rob gathered them all together to tell them. What was real was that Their Beloved Boys were moving on.

Grown men now, Rob and Tom both cringe and recoil at that term, and what I say now as we leave this story, for one simple reason: it is just not in either of their natures to be singled out. In their view, kudos and credit belong to the Team, not to them. They prefer to let results speak for themselves.

And they do.

Rob Anthony did indeed answer The Call. He is now senior pastor at a thriving church in Lake Oswego. Happily married to Laurie, his "retirement" at thirty lasted about a month. Like all parents, they both have been going full speed ever since. High school and college age now, his kids are almost grown. They all play sports just like the "old man," but I haven't heard if any have been tossed out of games for a temper tantrum.

Tom Ross lives a mile from me in Little Rock. He didn't sit still very long, either. Tom went back to school and learned not only electrical engineering, but also surveying. He bought 80 acres of forestland before developers could grab it to build condominiums.

Instead, he turned it into a small, environmentally friendly community of homes nestled into that forest that was beautifully preserved. I was proud of him as a Green Hero, to be sure, but I still think he did it just to drive the contractor's heavy equipment.

Tom and Francie have raised three honest to goodness Eagle Scouts, and he spends his days close to his family, designing computerized security systems, doing consulting, and always quietly looking at the next possible entrepreneurial venture.

Tom and Rob did it. They lived the American Dream.

Their one Big Idea, saddled with their passion, optimism, honesty, integrity, and not a small amount of luck—all of these, along with more work than they ever would have envisioned, brought them to this bittersweet moment. They didn't just follow the 12 Steps of the Entrepreneur's Way; they lived them, and they got rich by living them. Tom did indeed make his million dollars by the age of thirty, and then some, as did his partner.

But in the end, the money has very little to do with their richness. It's what they became, and what they gave to others that made each of them a success. As I looked around the room during their Goodbye Party, I couldn't help but be taken again by the Butterfly Effect of these two "young and inexperienced engineers" deciding to start a company seven years before in that cracker box office up the road.

Paula and Lue worked far above and beyond the call of duty in getting these guys through the most difficult days of their young lives. In exchange, they will tell you that they had their faith restored - faith in people, and faith in themselves.

Vic Risley didn't just get a new income stream as a manufacturer's rep. He became a mentor to a young man. He literally helped Rob not only become a better salesman and speaker, he changed untold numbers of lives by further preparing Rob for the work of his life, being a minister.

Bud and Clint weren't just a little shop helping out these two kids anymore. They were a thriving machine concern now, their business positively exploded along with Anthony-Ross.

Todd departed from the path of the corporate engineer, and got to help fundamentally build a company that he would ultimately run three times longer than the original partners did. Joining Tom and Rob literally changed the trajectory of the Anthony-Ross Company and Todd's professional life.

And Byron, well the quirky, hourly employed millwright was that no longer. He made plenty of money thanks to the deal he signed with these two, enough to build a new house with a bigger shop, get the kids through college, and make sure he and Nancy could retire in comfort. But far more, he'd been validated in his work as the conceiver and original inventor of an industry-changing device that set this whole thing in motion.

With many a tear, Tom's old man and advisor to them both joined in the toast… to two guys who lived the American Dream, and to each of us who was richer because of it.

Book Two

The CityForest Story

Now that we've looked at one successful American Dream in the Anthony-Ross Company, I want to notch it up a bit in our second case study and introduce you to another amazing story, that of Wayne Gullstad and CityForest Corporation. There are many similarities; same industry, same Entrepreneur's Way, and application of the 12 Steps in this man's business and life. You will even see a lot of Tom and Rob in Wayne.

However, the differences are obvious and profound. CityForest was a bigger and much more expensive and labor-intensive start-up and, as a result, far more difficult and complex at every stage. I linger on this difficulty, especially in the *internal* difficulty for the entrepreneur, as it is crucial to understand - starting and running any full-time business is not for the faint of heart. The bigger the idea, the harder it's going to be.

But patterns remain. Fundamentals still apply.

As you will see, the Principles of the 12 Steps hold true, whether it's a privately funded $75,000 engineering start-up built around marketing a single product, or something much, much bigger, involving a lot more people, a lot more money and, quite honestly, a lot more luck. See if you can spot the similarities, as well as the fundamental differences.

Enjoy the incredible but true journey of Wayne Gullstad and CityForest, a real life story of the American Dream.

Prologue

It was pouring. Mid-morning, but dark as night. No matter how furiously the wipers on Wayne Gullstad's truck slapped at the rain, they couldn't keep up. He couldn't see the Mill, but driving there, he could see police tape, cones, and a rain-slickered sheriff's deputy waving at him not to go further. It told him beyond any doubt that *it was bad*.

Rising water, as far as he could see, in every direction.

Wayne grew up in Washington State, and thought he knew rain, but he'd never seen anything like this Wisconsin storm. It had been dumping for two days, non-stop, sheets of water hammering this little Midwest town into a flood-zone. Indeed, the dam above the mill had broken upstream, and even if it was designed to flood to the side and not straight down river, the parking lot of the CityForest Paper Company was under two feet of water, and more was coming.

Wayne spun the truck around and raced to the back of the mill, where the structure itself was most at risk from the raging torrents, and slid to a stop. He threw his hood over his head, jumping out. "I gotta get inside, Cliff!" He shouted to Cliff Bieinart, his chief of operations.

"You gonna swim it, Wayne?" Cliff answered.

Wayne pointed at a boat paddling its way from the Mill. Two employees.

Five minutes and a treacherous parking lot crossing later, Wayne and Cliff crawled out of the boat and onto the partially submerged ramp leading into the Mill's basement. He forced a smile and a thumbs-up to the half-dozen guys who were going like hell, throwing up sandbags around the perimeter. He dashed inside, praying they'd held the water out.

They hadn't.

Wayne paused on the ramp, groaned silently at the sight of his Mill floor, like a man looking at the wreck of his favorite car. It was three feet deep or more in here, too. Hundreds of thousands of dollars worth of electric motors and machinery were half sunk in the brown water, giant rolls of paper now just soggy pulp again. Men in fishing waders did the best they could, but this battle was clearly lost. He considered ordering them to stop, but why? Sometimes, even futile action is better than standing by helplessly.

"Don't worry, Wayne," one of them shouted up to him. "We're not dead! We can save this thing!"

Wayne nodded stoically. This had been the year from hell. A fire eight months ago burned up 300 tons of paper, an accident claimed the life of an employee the summer before. They'd barely made payroll last week. The paper market was tanking while interest rates were spiking along with pulp and fuel costs. Customers were rejecting deliveries on quality control grounds, and nobody could find the problem.

Now a 200-year flood had the CityForest Paper Mill under water. The CEO, a 36-year old new father who launched this vision in the first place, restarting a mothballed factory, pledging every asset he had or ever would have to guarantee its financing, employing what seemed to be half of the town of Ladysmith, Wisconsin...

He felt like the idle equipment sitting quietly below him: *sinking fast.*

Chapter One
The Journey of Wayne Gullstad

If you'd met Wayne Jay Gullstad when he was in high school, you would have been hard-pressed to peg him as a future CEO. "I was not even remotely a leader," he recalls now. "I guess you could call me a jock wannabe, but I spent most of my time on the bench. I actually hung out with the slackers more. I definitely had some self-esteem issues."

Norwegian in ancestry, with the Nordic jaw line to prove it, Wayne was born to a father who was an adventurer, a drifter, and a serial entrepreneur. Fred Gullstad left high school to enlist in the Navy in World War II, and served as a Navy gunner flying bombing missions over the islands of Northern Japan. It was tough duty. Less than half the planes and men in his unit made it back. He studied a correspondence course between bombing runs and came home a high school graduate.

Fred was a big "idea guy," great with the Big Picture and even better with people. A born seller. Wayne remembers the inventor-entrepreneur perpetually just "this close" to the Big Score with one of his always-original ventures: a car-plane, a collapsible boat, a coat hanger with extendable shoulder supports, an auto plant in Saudi Arabia he actually pitched to King Faisal, a hand-held steam-powered wrinkle remover (for clothes, not skin). Creative, personable, enthusiastic, and very skilled in many areas, it seemed only a matter of time until one of the Big Ideas would hit.

But it never happened. Fred was not a detail guy. Even if he had good people skills, *managing* people was not something he was born to do, either. Worst of all, he wasn't particularly great at managing money. Any one of these liabilities can sink a venture. It's a testament to the sheer force of his will that he was able to survive all three. Fred moved from business to business, at times right on the brink of either great success or outright failure, viewing every financial gain as a signal to try the next big idea.

Wayne was born in 1958 to Doris (Mitchell) Gullstad. A farm girl from Alberta, Canada, Doris was the polar opposite of Fred, as risk-averse as he was a risk-taker. She worked her entire life. Sometimes, her income as a bookkeeper was the only thing standing between the Gullstads and financial collapse. "I distinctly remember," Wayne says, "Mom making 2 dollars stretch an entire week for us."

The only fights Wayne remembers his parents ever having were over money. Doris accepted one scheme after another over the years, but always feared the instability of it all. She was a coupon clipper who hated credit, and really hated creditors' phone calls.

The Gullstads were, by Wayne's own description, "just a step above poor." but since he and his sister never knew anything different, it was never truly an issue. In spite of fairly frequent financial stress, the Gullstad home was still a happy one. Both parents lavished affection, praise, and encouragement on Wayne and his sister, drilling into their heads that they could do virtually anything they set their minds to, so long as they were willing to work for it.

The high school "self esteem issues" Wayne remembers are surely the result of a frequently absentee dad, or worse, sometimes actually "working for" Dad. Both possessed strong opinions, competitive spirits, and the stoic, granite-like stubbornness for which Scandinavians are famous.

Yet, some of Wayne's best and most important lessons as a man and a future entrepreneur came from moments with that Dad on fishing and hunting trips, just the two of them. In the forests and streams of Washington State, Fred would let his guard down a little, talk to his son, not as a boy, but a man. A contemporary. He'd share his latest venture, the inevitable ups and downs of business, the values of truth, service and reliability, and a man being only as good as his word. Lessons the boy would take into manhood and put to the test soon enough.

Sadly, the father wouldn't be around to see the lessons put to those tests. Fred Gullstad died of a heart attack in 1980.

Wayne is tall now, but he wasn't then. He loved sports, but never truly excelled at any until he discovered wrestling his senior year. As a student, he was a tad above average. Bright enough, school just never stimulated the boy, and he didn't find it very challenging. Besides, he would have rather been fishing, playing sports, or making money any day, over sitting in a classroom listening to a high school lecture that seemed to have zero relevance to any of these interests.

Wayne definitely got the Big Idea thing from his Father. He is a born entrepreneur. Like Fred, he always worked, but there was one distinction, and it was obvious early. Wayne had a *knack* for making money. Even at age nine, he had the innate ability to analyze a market and adjust his business plan accordingly. After starting his first venture collecting bottles and turning them in for deposit money, Wayne quickly saw a superior market for recovered golf balls from the local courses. This was a better investment of his resources (time and youthful energy), higher price-point for his product (50¢ a ball over 5¢ per bottle), with less storage required. It was also a more cost effective way to bring his product to market; no capital required for his raw material, no producing, and his inventory replenished itself every day by golfers who put the balls in the ponds and woods of the courses at no charge to him (there's never any shortage of that, on any golf course). Wayne cleaned them up and sold them right back to the golfers who'd put them there in the first place, bringing an added bonus of customer satisfaction. The golfers, meanwhile, perceived themselves as savvy bargain shoppers who seemed to ignore the fact that they were more or less buying back the same ball they'd already bought, this time at only 50¢ apiece.

Bulletproof plan, until security issues closed the operation down. The greens keepers started chasing him off.

At ten, Wayne read a fly fishing book and started tying flies, hour after hour in the Gullstad's garage. He seemed to have a knack for this as well. Wayne's dad took one look at the flies and encouraged the boy to market them to the local sporting goods store, which he successfully did. It became a real business. Wayne learned how to ask for the order, produce and deliver on time, bill his client, and get the check.

It just about broke both Fred and Doris' hearts when Wayne announced he would not be starting college the fall after he graduated from Ingraham High. Not that they could have afforded it, it had simply been their dream that he would do so.

"Neither of my parents went to college. They were counting on my sister and me to be the first."

It just didn't make sense to Wayne, and he didn't want to incur a bunch of debt in student loans. Although he had no alternative plan and no prospect beyond continuing as a stock-boy/janitor at Woolworths, and knew he wouldn't exactly be the cream of the hire-able crop with only a high-school diploma, it was actually a very rational and responsible decision for an 18-year old boy.

"I didn't have the vaguest idea what I wanted to do with my life, or even what to study," he says now. "It just seemed a complete waste of time and money, starting college because you didn't have anything else to do."

What he did, of course, was go to work full-time, and herein lay the turning point of young Wayne Gullstad's journey.

There was a carpet-cleaning outfit nearby, and they were all too eager to hire a single, 18-year old with a car and an excellent work record. For over a year, Wayne consistently worked six day weeks, morning to night, running a carpet cleaner in homes and businesses. The money was decent for 1976, it worked out to about $1000/ month in straight commissions, but the actual job was, in Wayne's very frank words, "Horrible. Dirty, wet, repetitive, noisy, solitary, and going nowhere."

Now on the surface, this is the textbook definition of a "dead-end job," but dead-end jobs, I believe, may get a bit of a bum rap. Difficult and frustrating though it can be, there's ultimately a value to a repetitive, non-intellectual, and solitary employment like this, as it gives a person hours and hours to *think*. A young man or woman can, and usually will, begin to ask profound questions and come to even more profound conclusions.

Wayne Gullstad did just that.

First off, maybe without knowing it, Wayne asked and answered the Big Question, *Am I an Entrepreneur?* He'd already run his own businesses, had a very defined spirit of independence, and risk wasn't something he was afraid of. At eighteen, with nothing more than time to his name, he had nothing to lose! The boy was polite and respectful, but he'd long since come to the conclusion that he wasn't crazy about working for other people. He far preferred working for himself.

That point was driven home by a major part of his carpet-cleaning job description—*expanding the order*. Wayne was expected to show up on the doorstep of each customer who'd ordered the $32.95 basic cleaning, and proceed to sell them on a whole host of other services - drapes, furniture, spot remover, or even an upfront deposit on a regular scheduled service. None of these things of course is illegal or unethical, but they're not exactly straightforward, either. And it really bothered a principled young man, who'd had the virtue of honesty drilled into him since birth, to be told to hard-sell people who only wanted (and most times could only afford) the $32.95 rug cleaning service they'd called for.

As if that weren't enough to hasten a life decision, there was a personal discomfort here, too. Wayne hated hard selling anyone. It just wasn't in his nature. He may not have cared for pushing a heavy droning steam cleaner unit for 12 hours a day, but it beat pushing product and services on people who didn't need or want them.

"I remember this one job at the very end of my illustrious career there. I went through the shpiel and sold some little old lady living on not-the-best-side-of-town a whole slew of services. Spent the entire day there. As we were settling up when I finished, I just couldn't do it. I charged her what she called us for, $32.95, and that was it. The rest was on me, I didn't care if my boss took it out of my check. I just wasn't gonna do this to people anymore. Maybe college wasn't such a bad idea after all."

Wayne quit the carpet cleaning business for good and, to the delight of his parents, enrolled in community college. He knocked out his required courses, made the grades of a far more mature young man who's been out in the real world long enough to learn the lessons it teaches, then transferred to the University of Washington and asked himself the Second Big Question every Entrepreneur Must Ask:

What do I like to do?

No, I did not ask what do I *want* to do, or what do I *need* to do. The answers to those questions change a hundred times in life, and rare indeed is the 20-year old who can answer either one with authority. Oh sure, there are always some kids who know early on that they want to be doctors, lawyers, engineers, preachers - thank Heavens. The world wouldn't run nearly as well as it does if we didn't have this focused and driven minority. Contrary to popular opinion, they really are a minority.

As we did in Book One, let's go back to the data. A recent Gallup survey found that less than 20% of college graduates end up working in the career they chose as a major field of study. Think this is a skewed question, or more a function of the marketplace than an individual's choice, or even an exaggeration?

Okay, do something for me. Go to your local college and see how many kids are in the undergraduate "Liberal Arts" fields (English, History, Sociology, Languages, General Business) versus those in professional programs (Engineering, Law, Medicine, etc). It's something like 10:1, on average, by the way.

Now, hang out outside the Liberal Arts area and take your own random sampling. Ask every student you can, "What do you want to do with your life?"

Before campus security removes you, you will have accumulated more than enough data of your own. The answers will range from "Make money/Get Rich" to "Oh, I don't know, work in marketing or sales," or "Teach, maybe."

The honest ones will look you straight in the eye and tell you "I don't have the slightest idea," and there's nothing wrong with that. This is okay. It's normal! Look, let's just all come out of the shadows on this one. Most of us haven't got a clue, certainly not between the ages of 18-21, what it is we want to do with our work lives.

But we all know what we *like* to do.

This takes us right back to the 12 Steps of the Entrepreneur's Way. <u>Passion</u>. I care about what I'm doing. It is front and center in my career choice - *I like to do this. I like this world I'm hanging out in.* It's quite okay if that changes. Chances are excellent that it will! As over-generalized as this may sound on the surface, this is the foundation of succeeding at anything in this life. Start with this question:

Am I doing what I like to do with my days?

So, as Wayne Gullstad was flipping through the course catalogue of the University of Washington, before he'd even sent in his application, he asked himself that very simple but profound question. *What do I like to do?* He loved to fish, he loved to hunt, and loved being in nature.

That was it. No grand entrepreneurial vision, no exciting business plan, or even a job he was focused on at this point. Wayne just liked to be outside, and so he let his interests guide him. He chose Forest Management as his major, figured he'd figure it out from there.

When Wayne graduated in 1982, the United States was at the trough of one of this country's worst recessions. The job market was awful for everybody and forestry was no exception. Interest rates were sky high, timber prices hit rock bottom, housing starts were nearly non-existent. The US Forest Service and the wood products industry were laying off people in the thousands. Nobody was hiring anywhere. Finding a job in this kind of economic downturn was going to be needle in the haystack stuff.

Sound familiar, 2009 grads?

It clearly wasn't going to be a simple matter of scheduling interviews, sending out resumes, or going to a job fair. In his initial exploratory phone calls about possible job openings, Wayne was literally laughed off the phone more than once.

What he may have lacked in timing and luck, Wayne made up for in the working and sports experience of his youth, and being the son of a lifelong entrepreneur. Three things (a positive approach, tenacity, and the ability to visualize) all came together in a very simple creation that fueled him on when most anybody else would have just thrown in the towel and chosen another field.

"My sister taught me this in high school. You make a poster, cut out pictures of what you like to do, what your dream job would be. Mine had people climbing in the Cascades, guys hanging off harnesses at the top of 100-foot Douglas Firs, tracking wildlife, and kayaking through Class Four rapids," Wayne laughs. "I know it sounds a little juvenile, but I am telling you, it works. Talk about inspiring! I looked at that thing every single day, and just said, *I want this!* So I wasn't afraid to cold call anybody - not if they could get me there."

Always the strategist, Wayne compiled a list of 22 questions he'd want to ask any executive or decision maker in this business, and started calling company presidents and vice presidents, requesting a meeting, either in person or by phone. He was sincere in his approach, shot straight with each, telling them he understood how depressed the market was, but that he fully intended to work in this business, no matter how long it took, and just wanted the benefit of their wisdom and experience.

"I never got turned down," he says today, then corrects himself. "But there was this one executive at Burlington Northern...."

The Company President stared incredulously at the 23-year old. "Exactly who are you again? And how did you get my name?"

"My name is Wayne Gullstad. I was referred to you by Mr. O'Leary, and requested this meting through your secretary and—"

"What is it you want?"

"Well, I'm interested in a career in this field and —"

"Oh for gods sakes, son, just go to Personnel and fill out an application, can't you see how busy I am?"

Wayne was undeterred. "Sir, I'm here because your office confirmed this meeting. All I'm asking is for a little of your time, that's all."

"You got ten minutes."

"Thank you." Wayne began. "First off, what is your educational background?"

"What...? What the hell business is that of yours?" the president roared and flew off the handle at Wayne's impudence in "...barging in here on a work day to ask me a bunch of personal questions! This 'interview' is over!"

I said Wayne is personable, respectful, and rather stoic, but he isn't a doormat. After about a minute of dressing down and a host of general insults, he'd had enough.

"Look," he boldly interrupted this very, very powerful company president, who probably hadn't been interrupted in years, "You're in the type of business I'd like to be in someday. If I don't know how **you** got here, how the hell will **I** know how to get here, and what to do when I **am** here?"

The guy stopped and laughed softly. There was no denying, the kid had a backbone. "I guess you have a point, son."

Ten minutes later, Wayne kept his word, thanked him, and ended the meeting. "No, no. Sit down." The executive stopped him. "I still have some time."

Tenacity aside, things were bleak out there. Even if he did win this very powerful executive over personally, the guy simply didn't have a job for him.

Wayne was running out of money. He drove up and down Interstate-5, Highway 101, and every other road in the Pacific Northwest that might have a timber mill, a paper plant, or a forest to manage. He slept in the camper on his Datsun pick-up. The lowest point was cracking a cylinder head in the middle of Oregon, and coughing to a stop in front of a church. It was his address for a few days. He didn't have the $178 to fix it. Neither did his Mom when he called home.

Fred had died two years before and Doris was struggling to make ends meet. He wasn't calling for money anyway, he just wanted to say hi and talk to his Mom. Lucky he did, because Kelly Services had called that afternoon, inquiring if he was interested in a Temp Job in Oregon—not far from the phone booth he was calling from! ('83, no cell phones).

Timber giant, Crown Zellerbach, just down the road in Wilsonville, Oregon, was offering $7.50/hour for conducting "research" at the 300-acre facility they leased from Boeing, growing poplar trees for paper pulp. In reality, the "research" was little more than hard, manual labor. Digging and laying irrigation lines, clearing brush, fixing pumps and filters, trimming trees, measuring growth…

Wayne absolutely loved it. It may have been dirty, difficult, and low paying work, and as a promising recent college grad perhaps he was way "overqualified" for it, but it was outside. Working in nature, *doing everything he liked to do*! The harder the work, the more it energized the young man. Instead of collapsing into his bunk in exhaustion at night, he would stay up, drafting proposals for new research and development programs to present to his employer. They were good, solid, well-written plans to improve their operation, and increase both output and profit margin for growing these trees for paper pulp, but they were dismissed out of hand. Never seriously considered. It was quickly obvious to Wayne why.

Wayne had detected some patterns in both his executive interview process and now working in the industry, and two of them were front and center as he pondered the brick wall he was encountering. There was a very defined class system here. All these guys had either sales backgrounds or a Masters in Business Administration.

Research Directors with PhDs are not fond of $7.50/hour temporary employees suggesting improvements to their programs (even when they happen to be right!). One even warned him to stick with his job, as "we're not paying you to think." It suddenly became obvious to Wayne. If he were going to be taken seriously and go any further in this industry or any other, really, a simple bachelor's degree wouldn't cut it. He would have to go to the next place in his education, or stay at this level of employment.

He picked up a syllabus from the University of Washington's Business School, bought the books on the list, and went to work on a self-directed MBA. He'd show up at Crown Zellerbach at 5:30 on the dot every workday, study for an hour and a half, and clock in at 7:00. Home at night, he'd crack the books again, same on the weekend. He kept this up for about a quarter before deciding he was going to pursue this for real.

Wayne applied and was accepted into UCLA's Business School. He packed the Datsun and headed for Los Angeles in the fall of 1984.

Chapter Two
The Education of a CEO

The Chinese Consul scribbled notes rapidly, copying figures from a document in his hand. "Go on, Mister Gullstad" he urged.

It was an incredible scene. Wayne hadn't even expected to get the official on the phone. This was only a UCLA Business School project. Here he was at the end of his first year, sitting in the Consulate of the Peoples Republic of China in San Francisco, pitching an idea to their #3 guy in America, beneath the Chinese Ambassador himself. And it wasn't a polite audience the guy was giving, the Consul was listening intently.

"Well sir, as you can see in my proposal, to ship logs from North America to China, have one of your manufacturers produce the plywood, then ship back to the United States, costs relatively the same as doing it all right here."

"Then what is the interest in doing it?"

"We need the plywood. We have the timber, but labor is too expensive in this market. Your manufacturers have equipment that's old, but perfectly operational, and the United States is interested in expanding business opportunities with your country."

It was a good idea, and a compelling proposal. So good that the head of the program at UCLA funded Wayne's research as a Work Study, and arranged for the meeting with the Chinese Consul. Still, after a second meeting and another proposal filled with all sorts of corporate and government regulations data, the idea died a quiet death in red tape. That wasn't what perplexed Wayne. It was something far more basic... *Why is this guy taking me seriously?*

"I'm a student with no money, no expertise, or resources, and this official from the biggest country on Earth is taking a meeting with me," Wayne told Dennis Sinclair, his Entrepreneurial Studies Professor at UCLA after the deal was clearly dead. "Do you think he was a spy?"

"Maybe," the professor replied. "But did you learn anything?"

Wayne thought for a moment. He really wasn't sure that he had.

"Look. There's plenty of money, resources, and expertise out there, but very few great ideas to put them all to work. You get that and they'll all come to you."

"So all I need is just a great idea," Wayne completed the thought, smiling at the memory of his father Fred, the consummate "idea guy."

"That," smiled Sinclair, "And the stones to actually go for it!"

Of all the lessons Wayne Gullstad learned in the Graduate Program at UCLA, none was more valuable than this first Immutable Law of Entrepreneurship.

The First Immutable Law of Entrepreneurship

A great idea, plus the guts to go for it, and they will come to you.

This international plywood deal might have actually gotten done had the student pursued it. There were many reasons he didn't, but the biggest hurdle of all for Wayne was the inner one. He couldn't stop asking himself that question, *why are these people taking me seriously?*

You can see where he's coming from here. One of the highest-ranking foreign-service officers of the largest country on Earth is considering the proposal of young Wayne Gullstad; the ex-carpet-cleaning, irrigation ditch digging, Datsun camper shell driving, *student*!

I don't know if the guy was a spy or not, but a good idea is a good idea. Wayne's sudden indecision is the most common inner doubt we have to win in business, whether it's a full-blown conference room presentation or a cold call—*why is this person listening to what I have to say?*

There is an old maxim that on our road to success, we need to "fake it till we make it." That can obviously be taken to a ridiculous extreme. I really don't want my doctor or airline pilot "faking it." On the other hand, the good professor is absolutely right about one point: what separates the successful from the also-rans isn't necessarily talent and brains. Often it's just having the stones to get in the game and play it.

Believe me when I say this. I'm a former CEO. I listened to proposals and ideas for thirty years, and bought more than my share. I know from experience that a good idea with the gumption to stand up and own it - no matter who you are- is the surest way to "Yes."

UCLA was relatively cheap, as far as graduate schools go. Wayne found a room to rent in a quiet neighborhood close to campus, and adopted a very disciplined study schedule - disciplined, in that he wasn't about to study 80 hours a week. Los Angeles was too fun a place to be, and he wasn't about to miss this adventure by spending two years exclusively in a classroom and the library.

He had a barely functioning alarm clock, which would only go off only at certain times on the dial. One of those times was 5:22 AM. Wayne would rise then, shower and head to campus by seven, quietly study and focus for two hours, go to class, study some more in the evening, and quit by 10 PM. He kept a careful log of his time, and it reveals that he spent 40-45 hours working per week in class, studying or writing alone and in-group, attaining his graduate degree. Simple time management and discipline actually worked out to require fewer hours at the books than the average student would spend.

It was a diverse and interesting group, but Wayne found a lot of commonality here. With few exceptions, the students entering the program had spent at least two years in the professional working world before coming back to school. Many had left or put on hold careers as attorneys, teachers, nurses, engineers, you name it. He didn't find his fellow students over-the-top brilliant or elite in any way, but perhaps more focused and purpose-driven than those in other fields. It was a small distinction, but one that would ultimately drive Wayne to a place worth writing a book about.

And it is my Second Immutable Law of Entrepreneurship:

The Second Immutable Law of Entrepreneurship

Success isn't so much for the most brilliant and talented, but the one who can MANAGE the most brilliant and talented.

My co-writer, Howie Klausner, had the once in a lifetime opportunity to work with legendary actor-director Clint Eastwood in the production of the film *Space Cowboys*, from the screenplay written by Howie and Ken Kaufman. Not one to *waste* a once in a lifetime opportunity, when Howie got the chance to ask Mr. Eastwood the secret of his success, he didn't hesitate. Mr. Eastwood's answer to his question is very telling for us all.

Mr. Eastwood summarized his working philosophy and method as one of the greatest film directors in film history this way:

"I hire the best people I possibly can, tell them what needs to be done, then get out of their way, and let them do it."

I believe the product legacy of Mr. Eastwood in subconsciously following this Second Immutable Law speaks for itself. Not only has his pragmatic working philosophy helped produce some of the greatest motion pictures in our culture, it has created a loyal working unit that assembles time and time again to produce these motion pictures.

"That's the lesson here. Film crews are, for the most part, just random groups of professionals who happen to be available for a particular production," Howie Klausner tells me. "Not Malpaso (Mr. Eastwood's production company). Most of these folks have been with Clint for years, and it shows in the working environment, no matter what kind of movie they're making. That's the lesson here. They're not just his workers or his crew, they're his Team."

As you will see, this approach would become the foundation of Wayne Gullstad's managing philosophy. **Team.**

Wayne had noticed over the years that he was pretty good with numbers. It seemed the natural and obvious course to emphasize Finance in his studies at UCLA. It seemed even more natural to super-develop an area in which he was reasonably strong. This is time-honored, conventional wisdom. For a course of study whose ultimate measure of success is the *job* its graduate secures, it makes perfect sense. It is a smart choice to concentrate on one area of the larger subject of business. The corporate world loves labels, category boxes that people can accurately be filed under. And when that corporate world is hiring, it wants a category for their future executive: a financial guy, an operations woman, HR specialist, etc.

But this isn't a book about getting a job. This is a book about Entrepreneurs.

Wayne didn't have a career map or strategy laid out before him. At 28 years old, he had no idea he would be a CEO in three or four years. However, his instincts told him that whatever the job path, it would take him past simple numbers. He undertook a broader base of study, taking courses all over the business spectrum. He would actually graduate with enough units to claim an MBA degree "emphasis" in finance, marketing, and international business.

There were other areas of emphasis his definition of success would require.

Carol Lewis grew up in the San Fernando Valley, just over the hill from Los Angeles. Like Wayne, she also was the child of an entrepreneur, making money from an early age. Before she was sixteen, she'd had two successful ventures with her best friend, a car detailing business and a kid's party planning business. She started college at Penn's Wharton School of Business, but the weather was miserable that first winter. She longed for her native California climate. Carol transferred to Cal Berkeley, graduated with a business degree in Natural Resource Economics, and worked one year as a buyer for Clorox before heading to UCLA's business school.

It took about a day for Wayne to notice the attractive first-year student.

"I ended up in a study group with him and three other second year guys," Carol remembers. "Sounds like a real honor for a first year student, until I looked at them and realized this group was a bunch of engineers, which meant I'd be the one "honored" to do all the writing!"

Though Carol's writing ability was undoubtedly a recruiting factor, and Wayne certainly recognized a sharp business mind and a kindred entrepreneurial spirit, his interests slightly transcended those of Grad School. Even if he downplays his sales ability, he had learned the art of personal persuasion. She joined the group, and the two of them were steadily dating soon thereafter.

It isn't required for your degree to have a job set up by graduation, but let's just say it is strongly encouraged in MBA Programs. As his UCLA days were winding down, Wayne began the process of setting up interviews. It was starting to feel, as Yogi Berra famously described it, *like déjà vu all over again.*

The Forest and Timber Service companies still were not hiring. Not much, anyway. Wayne couldn't even get an interview with companies like Plum Creek Timber and Weyerhaeuser. Boise Cascade Paper Division was his first choice of prospects. He interviewed at their Portland Headquarters. No job offer.

Wayne had learned persistence over the years, so he jumped on the phone right away with the Senior VP of the paper company and wanted to know why Boise turned him down! Boise backpedaled after he declared his intention of working for this company, even if it was driving a truck! He should have been more careful with his declarations, as the next call came from Boise's facility in Rumford, Maine. Would he please come and interview for a job for their paper mill, *in the middle of nowhere on the other side of the country!!!*

Oh, man. I mean, the Boise guy did go out on a limb for him, probably forced the Maine Mill to interview him for a position they may or may not have even had open. However, the last thing this West Coast boy with a steady girlfriend was looking for was moving three thousand miles East.

Fortunately, Maine turned him down, too.

Wayne had two other prospects, Mobil and Hewlett-Packard. Though he liked Mobil, he was fascinated with the culture and business philosophies of H-P. Cupertino was close enough to LA to keep him in close contact with Carol until she graduated, and all indications were he'd get the offer. He flew up, had a great round of meetings and formal interviews...

And did not get the offer.

"Honestly, Wayne," the head of the interviewing committee told him when he called, seeking an explanation, "We were generally impressed. We just didn't think you were the smartest guy in the world."

Okay. Let me jump in here and make a quick observation. On the one hand, you have to hand it to the guy, he didn't lie to Wayne.

He didn't hold back. He called it like he saw it, shooting straight from the hip.

On the other hand, it he was working for me, he'd be out of a job that afternoon. I would have fired anyone on my staff who said that to a person seeking a job.

There are two things to point out here, and I want to make sure they don't slip by. First off, the guy was dead wrong. As you will soon see as this story unfolds, Wayne did not get short-changed on smarts. What I suspect is that the quiet, occasionally stoic countenance coming from his Norwegian DNA could come across as something lacking, in either intelligence or simple competence level. I would come to know later that nothing could be further from the truth.

Second, Wayne was unwittingly citing the Second Immutable Law of Entrepreneurship. Let me repeat it, because it really is that critical:

Success isn't so much for the most brilliant and talented, but the one who can MANAGE the most brilliant and talented.

This one's a toughie for most to swallow, because our egos get in the way, especially in the corporate world where the only true capital you usually have is the credit you get. We can't blame the corporate folks; that's the prevailing culture there, and in the world in general. Forbes and Fortune usually don't feature the quiet, non-rock-star, out of the spotlight managers, and executives, but they should. There are a lot more of them than you might think. Their code of conduct is what the young MBA interviewing at H-P aspired to be: a Team Player, who was far more interested in the successful results for his team, than who got credit for it.

I slugged it out in the corporate world for half a century. Trust me on this. This is rare thinking, but it is the stuff of true leadership.

"I don't know," Wayne laughs now, "Maybe I should have been offended. I think I was just blown away that anybody would even say that, but I shrugged it off. Hey, I needed a job."

Wayne called him back and pointed out that intelligence is not the only useful trait for a manager. He had other qualities that would probably value them as well, like honesty, integrity, a hard-working ethic, pretty much the entire 12 Steps list.

It apparently worked. The interview committee reconvened, and hired Wayne the next week as a financial analyst in their network software division.

And he…

Didn't like it.

The job was not the least bit interesting, or even enjoyable. It really just came down to one thing: they may have had a great corporate culture and cutting edge management philosophies, but he didn't find the product interesting, so he had no passion for it. As a guy who preferred trees and forests to microprocessors and office automation, he certainly saw no future in working there. H-P was and is a fine company, it just wasn't for Wayne Gullstad.

Besides, he'd just asked a woman to marry him, who was about to have her pick of some decent job offers herself. Wayne was perfectly willing to see where Carol's career would take her, and adjust his own path accordingly.

Carol Gullstad graduated in June of 1987, focusing her career direction on marketing. She received great job offers from both Kraft in Chicago and General Mills in Minneapolis. She and Wayne visited both cities, and decided Minneapolis was for them. She chose General Mills, where she would eventually head up the marketing of Yoplait Yogurt. Wayne gave his notice at H-P. At the beginning of summer, the couple packed up his camper and hit the road for their new life in the Twin Cities.

Chapter Three
Preparing

Minnesota may be known as the Great North Woods, but there really isn't much in the way of forests to be found without heading 100 miles north of Minneapolis. Wayne didn't expect a forest products job to appear close to their new home, and it didn't. He settled with a company in a related industry, the Waldorf Corporation. Waldorf manufactures recycled boxboard and corrugated cardboard. They also make folding cartons, like cereal boxes, supplying them to General Mills. Carol's new position there didn't hurt in getting Wayne an interview. He landed a job shortly after they arrived.

"My title was Financial Analyst," but what this position really afforded him was the opportunity to explore the full range of the paper and pulp business - from the inside of a large company. What would ultimately change the course of his life was one of his first on the job cash flow analyses, the company's use of waste paper.

Waldorf owned two paper mills, one in St. Paul and the other in Battle Creek, Michigan. Both mills used waste paper to manufacture boxboard, but they got their raw material in very different ways. Battle Creek purchased theirs on the open commodities market, already sorted, prepared and baled by the suppliers, and priced accordingly. St. Paul received their raw material, well, in the *raw*—300 tons of newspaper, magazine, and office paper and cardboard per day—dumped on a huge concrete slab in the back of the mill for processing and production, without the cost of sorting, preparing, and baling. Wayne didn't need his Finance degree to look at the numbers and see the huge savings and competitive advantage in purchasing waste paper this way, instead of on the commodities market.

Just a tiny bit of industry background: Waste Paper is more than just garbage; it is big, big business. This was not always the case. Matter of fact, it really took the Landfill Crises and the sudden realization that we were clear-cutting our timber forests into deserts by the 1970s for people to truly grasp that it really didn't have to be this way.

Those of us who remember the late 70s remember garbage barges floating up and down the Hudson River, with nowhere to land. The dumping grounds were full. Fully half of that garbage was <u>paper</u>, just looking for a place to go into the ground and quietly dissolve into the dirt. Meanwhile, back in the Pacific Northwest, trees were being cut at an accelerated rate. The timber companies were replanting and replenishing, but demand was simply going through the roof.

Please, spare me the anti-logging and timber industry attacks. It's not their fault the world's appetite for paper was (and is) growing exponentially every year. We need paper. Paper comes from trees, folks, and we're all in this one together.

Now, recycling used paper has been a do-able process for over a hundred years. But like so many things in life, be it energy or health or recycling, it usually takes some sort of a crisis to make human beings change their ways.

When we figured out in the 1970s that we were drowning in garbage and destroying our forests to keep up with our paper needs, we woke up and decided to make those changes. We got smart. We didn't do something silly like swear off paper and punish those who produce and use it. We looked at recycling the paper we were tossing into the landfills by the millions of tons per year. The success of this new way of thinking goes beyond the good feelings of being responsible and "green." It's profitable. The social and environmental good springs from that.

Companies were finally figuring out what had been in front of them all along: **recycling is a gold mine.**

Wayne Gullstad had figured this out already, and not from his graduate degree. You will recall, Wayne grew up recycling bottles and golf balls, not for the social responsibility of it, though that was of course a happy by-product. No, the ten-year old entrepreneur was doing it first and foremost for *profit*. It was only natural that recycling waste paper would catch his eye as well, especially after exhaustively studying it from every conceivable angle. For three years, Wayne focused on the acquisition, de-inking, and conversion processes at Waldorf, learning each side of the business from Tom Troskey. Tom was an exceptional business mind who understood the supply, process, logistics, economics, and competition of the paper industry.

Wayne learned well from his mentor, rolled up his sleeves, and put this knowledge to work for his company. Along with his duties as a financial analyst, he initiated several projects on his own. He proposed a joint venture with Waldorf and the manufacturer of Chinette brand paper plates, producing molded fiber products. He researched and proposed the construction of a de-inking facility for Waldorf. In discussions with Dick Nickel of Crystal Foods, a large egg producer, they began hashing out an idea to mix waste paper and chicken manure to make compost.

Now let's step out of the story for just a moment and recall Wayne Gullstad's journey from used golf ball peddler to carpet cleaner to Grad Student to Financial Analyst mixing chicken manure with yesterday's newspaper. What does any of this have to do with City-Forest, the company he would eventually launch, and the next-step subject of this book to begin with?

Thought you'd never ask.

Let me ask you a question. To borrow from a popular social networking internet site, *what are you doing right now*?

My gut tells me that most of you reading this story have not actually launched your entrepreneurial venture yet. You may or may not have your Big Idea. If you do, you're researching, thinking and talking about it, maybe reading a book about some folks who've gone before you. You're somewhere on the journey to Entrepreneurship, but chances are good you haven't taken the plunge just yet. You probably have a job or a commitment that takes up a fair amount of your time.

So here's my next question. *Are you preparing?*

Please understand, CityForest, the company that would define his professional life for seventeen years, wasn't even on Wayne Gullstad's radar in 1988. He was in his second year as a financial analyst, with no Master Plan. With more than twenty years hindsight, it's easy now to see the very logical path he was on, but he certainly couldn't see that then. I should note, even if he was a financial analyst, he didn't live and breathe numbers. He just happened to be pretty good with them.

Let me tell you then what Wayne *didn't* do.

He didn't fax his job in, occupying a position and title while looking for the first opportunity to jump away and start his own business somewhere. He threw himself into his work, served his employer, and learned everything he possibly could. He had no idea *how* he would ultimately use this new knowledge, but with an interest in any wood product derivative venture, knew that he ultimately *would* use it - somewhere, sometime.

At Waldorf, Wayne was living at #7 from the 12 Steps:

I Never Stop Learning.

When we look at Wayne Gullstad's journey in the days to come, we see him living this step out for his entire life, not just as CEO of CityForest. It's one thing to have the Big Idea. It's quite another to truly know your stuff. The learning never stops, and neither did he. As a result, when it was his turn at bat, he was ready.

And his turn was coming up fast.

Chapter Four
Vision Casting

It would be neat and tidy to tell you that Waldorf Corporation is where the journey hit full stride for Wayne Gullstad, the average kid from Washington. The guy who was searching for his purpose, finding it in this big paper company, putting all his passions, skills and learning to use in making them profitable and changing the world for the better, while climbing that corporate ladder at record speed.

Only it would not be remotely accurate. Not one of his proposals over five years was implemented by the company...not one!

"I don't blame Waldorf, or see them as short-sighted or cheap. They really weren't." Wayne looks back on it now. "The blame was mine. After all, they had the ability to make decisions and spend money. I just didn't make a very good case for any of these ideas. Now that I've actually run a company, I know. Coming up with an idea is easy. Doing it—that's the hard part."

The major disappointment was a particular idea of his that Waldorf was perfectly poised to adopt. It made great sense. The idea would have propelled the company to a leadership position in the industry and made them lots of money. It was a slam-dunk. For whatever reason, be it cash flow or a less than great presentation of his idea, Wayne failed to get Waldorf on board, even after 12 months of trying. Matter of fact, the executive he reported to effectively told him to cease and desist from the business development ideas and focus on his job, which was vaguely reminiscent of his boss at Crown Zellerbach telling him five years before he wasn't paid to think.

The hook was set. The "Big No" didn't deter or devastate Wayne, it only cemented the commitment to the Decision the stubborn Norwegian in him knew he would one day make. At 32 years old, he'd long since figured out that he had all three entrepreneurial traits in spades: a spirit of independence, a tolerance for risk, and a passion for this idea. And he'd done his homework. It was not only viable, it was something he could give his life to.

Maybe it was time to take the plunge.

On a quiet evening working late, Wayne sketched out a rough business plan and prepared his pitch for the smartest executive he knew. Someone at another company close by, in an unrelated industry, who would listen to his idea solely on its merits and give him an honest assessment on whether he should proceed. It just so happened he would be spending Thanksgiving with this executive the next week.

"Okay, let's hear it." The executive at the 'other company' sat back, ready to listen. Wayne cleared his throat, sat forward, and began his pitch for the company he was naming CityForest.

The Idea was to build and operate a stand-alone de-inking plant, which is exactly what it sounds like; a series of machines that removes all contaminants from recycled waste paper, the most prominent of which is ink, then sell the clean pulp to the paper-manufacturing sector.

His CEMO (Claim-Evidence-Method-Offering) was compelling:

> ▸ DEMAND: The Landfill Crisis had resulted in increased pressure on the manufacturers of paper products to use more recycled fiber.

▸ AVAILABILITY: The same crisis was driving huge increases in recycling efforts. Waste paper was cheap, abundant, and easy to get.

▸ THE MARKET: Paper. Huge. Enough said.

▸ COMPETITIVE ADVANTAGE: The "first mover" could lock down the major supply lines of recycled paper, and easily set up a customer base of companies like Weyerhaeuser, Boise Cascade, even Waldorf.

Wayne wrapped up his presentation, and watched the executive glance through the summary, processing the pitch.

"If this is so obvious and makes so much sense," the executive wondered, "Then why hasn't the paper industry done this?"

"Because it's change, and change happens very slowly in the paper business."

"How much money do you need?"

"A lot," Wayne smiled. "Still putting together numbers on equipment and construction. I just wanted your feedback on the overall idea."

"Well…"the executive smiled back, and closed the executive summary, nodding. "I guess you win, honey. Let's go eat some turkey and get started on your business plan."

Yes, the "executive from another company" was not only a very capable vice president on the fast track at General Mills, she was his new wife, Carol. They'd married in 1988, and she is a critical component in this story.

As the products of entrepreneurial parents, Carol and Wayne had made a slightly unusual "pre-nuptial contract" on their honeymoon: the first one to come up with the best business plan got to start that business, while the other kept their job and supported them in the meantime.

"I was actually working on my own business plan at the time I was about to present to Wayne so he'd keep his job to support my venture," Carol tells us now. "But as soon as I heard his idea, I knew that was it."

"Okay, Wayne. Let's go for it."

Now don't be fooled by the nonchalant-sounding "let's go for it." Carol had the same graduate degree in Business that Wayne did, and a vice president's title at one of America's premier corporations. She listened to his presentation with a lot more than just a devoted wife's ear - she ran it through a first rate education and an executive's due diligence process in analyzing a business.

Far more than that, Carol was well aware of at least some of the difficulty that lay ahead, how huge this task would surely be, and she could easily forecast that the odds of success were not in their favor. They'd been married going on four years when this venture began in earnest, and both were ready—excited—to start a family. Lastly, each had good, steady executive positions, making excellent salaries.

It was a good life the young couple had and Wayne was proposing to alter it dramatically. He was prepared to honor her answer either way, but wasn't at all surprised to hear her respond, "let's go for it."

Though she loved her career as an executive, Carol grew up in an entrepreneurial household. Her dad started and sold several businesses. The independent spirit was literally in her blood. She and Wayne had been searching for the "right thing" since business school. One of them was bound to find that "right thing" and take the other up on their original life-deal.

Most importantly, the obvious risks were not a deal breaker here. "I mean, let's be real," she laughs at the thought of it now. "We could have lost it all, and actually came pretty close to doing so."

Still, that thought didn't scare her off. "We were young enough, no kids, no big nest-egg at risk, I still had a job, and we both had

MBAs. What's the worst that could happen? The business fails? We lose everything? Okay. We'd just start again with something else."

I want to pause over this point and ask you to do the same. Because it is right here. As far as entrepreneurs go, we're separating the men from the boys, and the women from the girls.

More than any trait, step, or immutable law we've been discussing for this entire book, none is more critical than this: the willingness to take a risk.

Carol's statement above is not the norm. The possibility of "losing it all" is a chance most people are not willing to take, even at age 30, and childless. Once Wayne started doing the math on this new and groundbreaking venture, the initial excitement grew into the sober realization that he would need to raise or borrow upwards of $50 million. And, as the owner and CEO of this company, his name and personal property would be attached to that loan. The Gullstads have four children now, and they're not 30 any longer. I'm not convinced they wouldn't take the same chance today, but I can assure you the decision would not happen nearly so fast.

Yes, leaving a good corporate job and starting a company was a risk, but when you combine Carol's obvious talents, her business acumen, and her calm acceptance of this risk, you can see this was not exactly your run of the mill set of circumstances. In Carol, Wayne had more than a loving wife with a good job. He had a partner who was easily his equal in business, and most importantly, *a kindred spirit*.

It's this last one that is most critical, and I issue this as a cautionary word of advice to anyone out there married or about to be married, launching their own entrepreneurial venture:

Your chances of a happy day-to-day life are somewhat impaired if your life-partner is not equally yoked with your vision.

Most of us will not go through life with an MBA-holding, Fortune 500 vice president spouse who is "all in" with our idea to quit a good job and go hang it out there to the tune of tens of millions of dollars. No doubt about it, Wayne's situation was unique.

But the point with which I close this chapter is the most important of this entire book.

When Wayne was in college, a certain Business professor was asked the secret of having a truly significant career in business - in essence, the "Secret of Success." The professor answered that one's career must definitely come first, and the family second. It had to be that way, he maintained, if a full potential was to be realized, and the family would ultimately benefit most from one's reaching that full potential, at least monetarily. According to the professor, countless people had sacrificed what would have been spectacular success in business because they were held back by "the demands and commitments of a family."

As you are about to see, Wayne Gullstad is a born businessman and a gifted entrepreneur, but family was – is - *first* to him. He disagreed vehemently with the professor's position. Family does not represent "demands and commitment" in conflict with one's career. It is actually the **fuel** that drives it.

Wayne would not have gone another step in the business plan that would eventually become CityForest had Carol had not been on board, both as a businesswoman and his partner in this venture called life. He would have never succeeded in his ultimate goal: living a satisfying life that mattered, in partnership with his wife and family.

Fortunately, he had what he needed. Carol was on board. They'd settled into a comfortable but modest lifestyle and budget that could be sustained on just one of their incomes. For now, anyway.

The timing was as good as it would ever be. The couple shook hands and took the plunge. As 1990 came to an end, 32-year-old Wayne Gullstad resigned from Waldorf Corporation and set up his office in the spare bedroom of their house.

Now it was time to start a company.

Chapter Five
The Agreement

"Hello, is this Web Ross?"

"Yes it is. Who's calling?"

"Mr. Ross, my name is Wayne Gullstad, and you were recommended to me as someone knowledgeable about recycling and one who might be willing to help with a start-up company."

And so my path crossed with that of Wayne Gullstad, in 1992, in a phone call out of the blue. Six years after my first "retirement" and two years after the happy ending of the Anthony-Ross Company, I was living in Portland. Tom had moved to Arkansas where he was developing real estate. To this day, I think he was more interested driving the heavy equipment of the contractors than he was making money, and Rob Anthony had finished his training as a pastor and was working at a church in Atlanta.

And I was still too young to hang it up.

I had signed up with an executive search outfit. I wasn't looking for a job. I threw my name in there in case there might be another unique opportunity to advise, consult, or maybe invest in another venture in the industry in which I'd worked my entire life. The experience with Anthony-Ross had not only been profitable, it was a heck of a lot of fun. As a result, I was always listening for another opportunity like that.

Wayne asked if he could come to Portland to go over his business plan. He was smart enough not to give me any details over the phone. If he had, I'm sure I would have turned him down, but I agreed to meet with him, and we had lunch together near the Portland airport.

It was a good idea building a de-inking plant in the Midwest, but I thought Wayne was underestimating the enormity of the task. There were some major hurdles in his path, like:

Who were his investors? *He had some solid prospects, but none had written checks yet.*

How much money did he have? *He and Carol had saved a few thousand dollars, but that was a drop in the bucket compared to what he'd need.*

Where was he planning to locate this facility? *No idea. Hopefully near Minneapolis.*

"So let me make sure I understand you, Mr. Gullstad. Your plan is to raise the capital to build and then operate a 'green-field' (*from scratch*) de-inking plant to supply several mills. Is that the bottom line here?

"Yes sir," He answered.

"Do you have any idea of how much capital that really is?"

"Between 30 and 50 million."

"Sounds about right."

This was a huge undertaking. I wanted to turn him down right at this point, but his enthusiasm and obvious passion for this project were contagious. I had to hear him out. I was particularly excited to hear that he was an advocate of participative management - the Team philosophy of giving the person actually <u>doing</u> the job authority and responsibility <u>for</u> their job, something for which I also had a particular passion. He was very knowledgeable and expressed himself very well on this subject. There was more to this young man than I might have thought in that first brief phone call.

I had my share of misgivings, but I really wanted to help Wayne out. To tell you the truth, I felt like he had plenty of the right stuff.

Now that I'd spent a meal with him, I just didn't have the heart to turn him down and deflate his American Dream.

"I think it's a long shot, Wayne, but I want to help you any way I can. I'll be honored to advise and consult, but I will not invest any money."

The business plan for CityForest was a very good one. I was pleasantly surprised to see just how much due diligence Wayne had done.

He had enlisted a wide circle of advisors before I came on the scene: investment bankers, other entrepreneurs, and smartest of all, a new law firm specializing only in start-ups. Even better, Frank Vargas of Vargas & Associates agreed to defer their legal fees until the company was up and funded. This was huge, and not exactly a boilerplate arrangement. Attorneys are not known generally for their largesse, especially for a profit-making venture, but Frank Vargas was a true entrepreneur himself. He also recognized a good business plan, and a stubbornly tenacious man behind that plan. Betting on Wayne was a pretty good gamble in Frank's eyes.

Unfortunately, Wayne was nowhere even near the starting gate. CityForest would need a lot more than a good plan and great people advising him. It needed capital, and a lot of it. Unlike Anthony-Ross, this was not a case of funding two engineers and the development of an invention. This was an exponentially larger venture. It would involve finding a large site, constructing a heavy industry plant, purchasing machinery, and hiring more than a hundred skilled workers and managers. And that's before the doors open!

Wayne was, and is, the 12 Steps personified, but going from business plan to operating a company was going to be the equivalent of the Moon Shot. After a year of "fund-raising," the CityForest rocket was still firmly on the ground.

He'd begun the process by networking and identifying every potential source of money. "Angel Investors," typically wealthy individuals willing to invest $10-50 thousand dollars in a venture, were the primary focus at the start. His plan was well received, but it was obvious that it would take an army of typical angel investors to raise more than just seed capital.

The Venture Capital community was the next stop, but he didn't linger there. "They were all very generous with their time and more than willing to give me advice," Wayne remembers, "But CityForest was not their target investment. The VCs I met were looking for a big hit that would take off with a huge growth rate, so they could cash out in 3-5 years." Wayne's plan was heavy on the up front investment, and reached a plateau within a couple years. Its long-term numbers were good, but it was a slow and steady grower. It wouldn't be the right fit for the venture crowd.

Next stop in Wayne's financing search, "Incubators." Generally speaking, Incubators are funding sources for technology development, and receive their own funding from a variety of government and industry sources. The problem here was that Wayne wasn't developing a new technology; he was looking to utilize existing technology.

Lastly, there was the possibility of government financing. Once Wayne settled on a site for his de-inking plant, the state of Minnesota would gladly jump into the mix. This is business development, jobs, ancillary businesses, and tax revenue. Of course, they would be interested. However, the state's primary interest was in expanding the market for waste paper in Minnesota. This was not CityForest's interest. The federal government proved to be a dead end as well.

After our third round of coffee at the Portland Airport Denny's, I put the business plan down. "What's Wayne Gullstad's goal here? I mean, really, 10-20 year plan. What's that vision?"

Wayne thought a moment. "Web, the big picture is creating value. Recycling. Returning value to the shareholders, creating jobs, creating a new company culture, and being a good community partner."

"That's it?"

"That's it."

"What about you?"

"What about me?"

"An exit strategy, for starters?"

"I don't have one."

This was a very refreshing answer, I must admit, and the one I was listening for. Now I know the conventional "wisdom" is for entrepreneurs to begin with the end in mind. Have a goal for how much you want to get out of your business, how long until and to whom you want to sell, etc. I think there's value in setting goals and targets, but I'm not sure I go along with that conventional wisdom, especially when it comes to something of this magnitude.

This was 1991, the beginning of the Tech Boom. Before this decade was out, entrepreneurs would be selling ideas that were little more than word-pictures on cocktail napkins for seven figures. Slap a dot-com on the end of them and you could sell it for eight figures. CityForest's road would not be at all similar, in the best of circumstances. This was old-world, heavy industry, not a quick-hit start-up that gets bought by Google or Microsoft in a couple years.

This company was going to be Wayne Gullstad's life, and might possibly be the last great thing he would build in that life. If he'd had some complex investment strategy, or a big parachute payday for him and his investors at some future date in mind, I would have picked up the check at Denny's, wished him well, and gone home. I might have been too young to hang it up, but I was too old for that game. My world was comfortable. I'd done more than well enough in Anthony-Ross to call it a day as an advisor, and enjoy a healthy retirement of traveling and seeing the grandkids.

But I could see this young man meant what he said. He was bound and determined to see this vision come to life, to hell with the odds, and it was for all the right reasons: *Doing things that mattered, creating value for people. Creating something that would last long after he was gone.*

Life's too short <u>not</u> to jump in that game, every chance you get.

"Okay, Wayne. Let's start with your Board of Directors…"

Chapter Six
Lightning Bolts and Hammers

It would be a great study, if it were possible to access the database of all human ideas, to determine how many great ones came into being and how many faded into oblivion, victims of the grind and hammer of life. It is common to us all. The lightning bolt of inspiration hits us, whatever the project or vision, and we enthusiastically roll up our sleeves to make that vision into reality. This is truly the "juice" of human existence.

Oh, if we could only sustain that juice, the excitement and joy of that lightning bolt. It is equally, perhaps *more* common, for those ideas and visions to slowly die in the difficulty of bringing them to life. I would be willing to bet that the reader of these words has had more than his or her share of million dollar lightning bolts in this life, that have literally disappeared into the ether, covered over by the difficulty of the next steps, the busy-ness of life, or the gradual loss of that initial enthusiasm, which is inevitable.

The human math on this one is pretty consistent. The bigger the vision, the harder it will be.

Wayne Gullstad's vision was big, and oh man, it was gonna be hard.

Eighteen months after leaving his job, that's eighteen months of living on one paycheck, maxing out their credit cards, reworking the business plan, and pretty much eating "No" for breakfast, Wayne could be forgiven that gradual loss of enthusiasm, as well as some serious second thoughts. His days were spent mostly on the phone, in the corporate headquarters of CityForest, otherwise known as the guest bedroom of the Gullstad house, but those days were numbered there. Carol was expecting now, and this would soon be their newborn's room. Matter of fact, Carol was ready for that paint job Wayne promised, and the crib they'd ordered would be here soon. Without a big infusion of capital to go find a space in an office park somewhere, CityForest would have to endure a company downsizing and a move to the basement, adjacent to the washer and dryer.

Some days were spent with piles of papers at McDonald's. Starbucks hadn't gotten to Minneapolis yet in '92, if such a thought is even conceivable now. The concept of "mobile professional" was not as widely accepted as it is today, especially in the slightly surreal surroundings of Ronald McDonald Land. It didn't matter to Wayne. Sometimes we just need to be around other humans, even if they are on a giant play-set.

The days were not as productive as he might have hoped, and actually had planned. Truth told, in his mind, Wayne had been confident at the end of 1990 that this venture would be up and funded in that first six months, a year at the outside.

Nearly two years later in 1992, he wasn't even close.

It isn't in Wayne's nature to ask for money, even believing as he did, and committing his very life to the vision of CityForest. This, by the way, is as common as that lightning bolt idea fading away in the face of difficulty. Very few of us are comfortable asking for the order, the investment… the *money*. It is our secret fantasy that our idea or venture is so great, the money will come to us.

But folks, it doesn't. Ever. Which leads us to…

Immutable Law of Business #3

If you ain't got it, you're gonna have to ask somebody.

The mountain is not coming to you, is what I'm saying. Unless your lightning bolt idea hits you when you are flush with lots of disposable cash, you're going to have to go to that mountain, and climb it. You will have to ask for money.

This was the reality Wayne was facing every single day. The mountain was not at all coming to him because, again, it doesn't. The Venture Capitalists weren't interested in his vision, the angel investors found it too big, the banks weren't lending, and the government would only help if they dictated the business plan and very nature of his company. There would be no financing this early stage of CityForest with the "traditional sources."

This is the grind and hammer of life for an entrepreneur, and where most of these ideas die. It's also a gut check. What are you prepared to do in this circumstance? It is this next-level question that demands an answer when the going gets tough, as it inevitably does. *How badly do I want this?*

If Wayne was going to see CityForest come to life, he was going to have to step out of his comfort zone. If you think he was queasy asking professional investors and lenders to invest, imagine the realization of his last resort for seed financing: friends and family. Wayne had long before sworn off the prospect of asking his friends to invest in any entrepreneurial venture. It was just too awkward for him - distasteful, even. There was nothing he dreaded more.

But now he had no choice.

There is an old saying we all know. "It's not about the destination, it's about the Journey." Here's another favorite of mine to go right along with it. "Do what you fear, and the death of fear is certain."

Wayne's fear and loathing of asking for money is hardly unique. Most everyone feels that way, at least once they are of age. It is fascinating, on the other hand, to watch children, who possess no such fear and loathing. I have eight grandchildren. Not one of them ever hesitates to ask me for a glass of water when she's thirsty, to go get a cheeseburger when he's hungry, and every so often, for a buck or two just because... they want some money.

What is it about children that they will simply state their need and ask for what they want? Yes, they are so young that the world hasn't yet had the chance to steamroll them or their idea with a few thousand "No" answers. True. But their expectation is that they get what they want when they ask for it.

In the case of their grand-dad, their success rate is about 100%.

In the case of their parents, the answer might initially be "no," but when they persist, or better yet, find a more effective way to ask or even strike a bargain, the rate is similar.

Now I know this is a business book, not a parenting guide, but stay with me. The key principle above is, *we get what we want when we ask for it.* Eventually.

This is the secret every great salesperson and entrepreneur knows, either consciously or unconsciously. Steve Jobs had to ask for money to get Apple off the ground. Same with Bill Gates, when he started Microsoft. Henry Ford? Yep. And the Hall of Fame list goes on and on. Wayne Gullstad would be no exception when it came to CityForest.

Now don't get me wrong here. Wayne knew very well he could never raise $30-50 million in his social and family circle. This was only seed capital he was seeking at the beginning. Many of the friends who would eventually invest in CityForest, like me (yes, I broke my vow not to invest), he didn't even know yet. This was going to be a process. In the case of Wayne's "Journey" thing, a very necessary process. It would not be easy, or comfortable, and it would not provide anywhere near the necessary funding to build and start up a de-inking plant and paper mill.

But it would be a start. And more than the comparatively small sum he would raise, one individual investor at a time, the value of this difficult but critical step in Wayne's journey would be clear over time. Facing and defeating this fear would be just as important to the success of CityForest as his original lighting bolt idea.

One last point on this. One of Wayne and Carol's close couple-friends read the CityForest business plan early on and wanted to invest $5,000 in the first round of seed financing. Wayne refused, at first, on the basis of his "friends and family off-limits" stance. *Why? How awful would we feel if our friends lost money on this?*

However, the couple pushed back. They were investing in a venture; they weren't giving out charity. This was a lot more fun than a mutual fund! They understood the risk, could handle losing the $5 grand - didn't want to, but could handle it - but most importantly, they believed in the plan, and they wanted in!

Their argument was very telling. If it's such a worthwhile and potentially profitable vision that you're gambling your own time and treasure, Wayne, why would you deny your friends the same opportunity?

Wayne very wisely relented, and took on the couple as first round investors.

But it would be a long haul, 5-50K at a time. With no location or site picked out, and no team yet to speak of beyond a handful of investors and a couple advisors, these were long days and nights between the spare bedroom, the basement, and the local McDonald's.

Wayne needed something to change. Fortunately, it was about to.

Chapter Seven
When Luck Comes to Call

Wayne is nothing if not thorough and methodical. If he was going to have to go through the process of pitching and asking people for investment, he was going to learn as he went along, and get better at it.

"Every time I'd get a 'No,' which was most of the time, by the way, I wanted to know why. I really did. Not arguing or challenging, I wanted them to help me get better at either the presentation or the plan itself. If there were flaws I didn't see, I wanted to know what they were."

One of the most consistent flaws he heard wasn't his presentation skills, or even his idea. It was the sheer size and scope of building a "green field" mill and starting up a brand new business from scratch. There were some near-misses. Boise Cascade and Lake Superior Paper were just two of several companies trying to increase their use of recycled paper in their product, and studied Wayne's proposal seriously. But time after time, whether it was a set of federal and state hoops that was just too time and capital-consuming, or the ever-present political dynamics of a large corporation; all turned out to be false starts. Yet, if nothing else, at least his pitch was getting sharper.

It was in the middle of this "pitching and listening tour" that Wayne found himself in a restaurant in Hudson, Wisconsin, with an executive at paper giant Pope and Talbot. Wayne's purpose in the meeting was to chat about CityForest and take this guy's temperature about possibly coming on board for a vice president's job, if he ever got CityForest up and running that is. Sometime between the burger and fries and after-lunch coffee, the executive dropped a bombshell that turned out to be an unbelievable stroke of #8 in the 12 Steps: *LUCK.*

"I think we're about to close the mill up in Ladysmith, actually."

Wayne froze, mid-creamer pour. "What?"

"It's not public knowledge yet and, please, you didn't hear it from me, but it's gonna happen. The thing just keeps losing money."

Wayne couldn't shake hands, say goodbye, and get to his car fast enough. His mind was racing ahead of his motor heading back to Minneapolis.

Ladysmith, Wisconsin - seventy miles north of the Pope and Talbot mill in Eau Claire. Tissue plant, already constructed, viable labor force. Easier to convert an existing mill to a de-inking plant than start from scratch, permit process would be smoother, investment would be much cheaper, not to mention far easier across the board.

He could scarcely believe it on June 4, when his call to Peter Pope, chairman of Pope and Talbot in Portland Oregon went through.

"This is Peter Pope. Who am I speaking to?"

"Mr. Pope, this is Wayne Gullstad. I'm the CEO of CityForest Paper here in Minneapolis. It's come to my attention that you might be considering closing your mill in Ladysmith, Wisconsin."

The silence was deafening… "Well, Mr. Gullstad, you are correct. I'm not sure how you found this out. What interest is this to you?"

Wayne outlined his business plan in under a minute, a direct benefit of his "listening tour" of investment pitches. And Pope got it.

"That's not a bad idea, Wayne. I'm gonna put you in touch with Mal Belafronto, head of our consumer products division, on one condition."

"What's that, sir?"

"This has not yet been announced, and these things are sensitive. This needs to stay quiet for the time being while we take the necessary steps."

Mr. Belafronto called the very next day. Wayne detailed the plan, with a brief summary of his background and his general interest in locating a de-inking mill in the Upper Midwest. "Since Mal didn't ask any questions about CityForest's operations, financial capability, or other personnel," Wayne says now with a smile, "I wasn't about to offer anything up."

He would have to wait for the news to become official, as well as the state and federally mandated plant-closing notices to be issued to the workforce and the community. Only then would a visit to the mill be arranged. Two weeks later, he made the two hour and forty minute drive from Minneapolis to Ladysmith Wisconsin, and drove onto the Pope and Talbot Mill grounds for the first time.

Ladysmith, Wisconsin is a town of about 4000, a farm and factory community, somewhat typical of the upper Midwest. Nice town, good, hardworking people. The mill sits elegantly on the banks of the Flambeau River, looking much as it has since its opening more than a hundred years ago; rock and mortar foundations, brick structural archways, and the massive, powerful and loud machinery of papermaking. When Wayne arrived on June 15, the mill was operating at near capacity, churning out what was expected to be the last production run of over a century's worth of paper and tissue.

What Wayne would remember most was the "look" from the employees working their shift that day—those that *would* look at him, that is. There had been plant closings before, changes of ownership - some good, some not so good. Many of the folks working that day had been through at least one.

This one was different. This wasn't a delegation from Kimberly Clarke or Boise Cascade arriving on-site. This was a young guy nobody had ever seen, or even heard of. Quite frankly, the guy looked pretty green.

It was obvious that nobody here was feeling good about this closing - this opportunity for the young entrepreneur from out of town. The feeling was downright palpable. These people were wondering if their mill would ever run again.

Wayne remembers their 'look' as "…a combination of fear, disappointment, anger, and skepticism, and not a lot of hope. I think it was at that moment that the magnitude of what I was attempting set in, and how costly failure would be to these people."

The next step was to sit down with Pope and Talbot, and figure out what this thing would cost. I was on the scene by now, had flown in to join Wayne on his next plant visit. Since P&T's headquarters weren't even a half hour from my house in Portland, I was happy to accompany him when he came to talk seriously about purchasing the Ladysmith Mill. I'm not sure my presence did much more than offer Wayne a tad more credibility from my own thirty years in the business, but maybe my being there made these guys assume Wayne had the financing and infra-structure behind him. I can't recall one question about CityForest's background and resources and, like Wayne, I wasn't about to offer up anything if they didn't ask.

The replacement value of the Ladysmith Mill - plant, machinery, buildings - was right about $50 million. Replacement values are important for insurance companies, but they don't mean much in a sale like this. Fortunately for Wayne, there were no other serious offers on the table for the mill, and there might not ever be. The Pope and Talbot mill had been losing money for some time. Ladysmith is not exactly the hub of any major industry, and the paper market wasn't exactly roaring right now.

That, in effect, could have made its value near zero.

But of course they weren't about to give it away. The consensus around the table at the end of the meeting in Portland was that Pope and Talbot would let the mill go for somewhere around $5 million. Wayne had succeeded in lining up some investors, and had lent CityForest thirty grand of his own money. Still, he was a bit shy of their asking price of five million.

He needed about another $4.9 million to shore it up.

Suddenly, after the despair of a barrel-of-nothing for eighteen months, this thing was falling into place, but Wayne was on the clock. He knew this opening would go away the minute somebody else showed up with $5 million.

Wayne got home to Minneapolis, and kicked the CityForest Fundraising Drive into *Over*drive. He burned the phone lines up, starting again with the "angel investor" crowd - $5 million is a whole lot easier to raise then 50! Every single person he knew in the paper business heard from him. He went back to the banks, and made contact with the state of Wisconsin for their participation. Before July was out, he'd had his lawyers review the Private Placement Investment Memo he'd written, and together they pored over the mill's financials. He even met with the plant manager, head of production, and the local union guys there. He was on the phone with Pope and Talbot every day. Some prospects were industry executives, like myself. He was no longer shy about asking for an investment, and equally bold about asking for advisement. A few investors became board members along with me.

The typical day of the entrepreneur at the fundraising stage of his company? A 504 mile round-trip drive to pitch to an investor prospect over lunch. The entrepreneur buys, by the way, followed by days and weeks of follow-up, at least one more drive over, maybe meet the investor at the plant two and a half hours away for a tour. All to land $20,000. Sometimes he got it, most times he didn't. One guy closed the deal at his car dealer's service bay, shaking hands and handing Wayne a check for $20 grand while his Cadillac was coming down off the rack.

By September, Wayne had raised more than $340,000 of first and second round investment, and was distributing the Private Placement Memo to institutional investors.

But he still needed to come up with more than 4 and a half million, just to have a shot at purchasing the mill.

As 1992 wound down into December, two years after he'd left Waldorf Paper and decided to take the plunge as an entrepreneur, Wayne had acquired five more graduate degrees' worth of knowledge about business plan writing, sales, finance, investment memos, and buying an existing business. He had grown exponentially as a person and as a businessman.

But the momentum of six months before was slowing to a stop, and he wasn't even close to realizing his vision of CityForest Corporation.

There is a small notation in Wayne Gullstad's day-planner on December 13, 1992: "Cancel all meetings."

It was with the usual mixture of emotions that Wayne first greeted his daughter Hailey Gullstad, born that day. As he held the tiny, bundled child in his arms, he was overcome with joy, of course, but suddenly soberly aware that he was responsible for one more life in this world. There's not a man anywhere who's held his first-born that hasn't felt this curious mixture, and said some sort of prayer not to blow it.

It had been a long and rough road for two years, and it wasn't showing any signs of smoothing out. Wayne was not taking a salary from CityForest's seed financing. Every penny of Carol's paycheck was going to their mortgage and their living expenses. Anything left over went into the business. They were even paying people out of their own pockets and credit card advances. Carol had never complained, never cast a doubt on their plan. She was his partner in this venture as much as she was in life. If she was worried, she never showed it.

However, they were no longer the same people who shook hands and said, "let's go for it." They were parents now. The way things were going, there was no margin for error, accident, anything. Lord help them if something went wrong.

Suddenly the concept of risk was very real.

Now holding his baby, Wayne was very clear. He couldn't go on like this. He had to know one way or another. Is this really going to happen? If not, he needed to get out – **now**, pay back his investors any way he could, get a job, do whatever he had to do.

Driving home from the hospital alone that night, Wayne had flashes of his own Dad, and some of his ventures that didn't work out. His mother making $2 dollars stretch for a week. Creditors' phone calls. Wayne wasn't even sure they could afford to keep this baby in diapers!

No. This was unacceptable. Failing at a start-up would be painful, but failing as a father and provider was simply not an option. By the time he had turned onto his own street, he realized just how exhausted he really was. As always happens when a man is dog-tired, his inner voice began laying out a convincing case that this was all for naught.

Nothing was worth this. He was missing his life in this uphill climb, regardless of all the wonderful personal growth as an entrepreneur. This whole enterprise was putting way too much pressure on Carol. He didn't even want her to have to work, and here she was going into Year Three of supporting both of them! Now they were three. All these people saying no. Maybe Wayne was just too Norwegian-stubborn to see that his Big Idea was impossible.

And even Pope and Talbot. They weren't idiots. They'd long since figured out where Wayne was. They were just humoring him until someone else—*anybody with cash!*—came along, and they'd forget they'd ever even heard of a company called CityForest. Why would this big company even give a rip about some guy in the middle of…?

Wayne hit the brakes as he pulled into the driveway. His head-lights swept across the front porch, where four huge cardboard boxes blocked his front door. He dashed up the stairs and tore open the envelope glued to the top of the largest box. The card read,

Welcome Hailey, and Congratulations Carol and Wayne! Your Friends at Pope and Talbot.

The four boxes were six months' worth of diapers, one of P&T's best selling consumer products.

He sat down on the porch, unable to blink back the tears welling up in his exhausted eyes. It was gonna be okay. No matter what, life goes on.

And went straight to bed, sleeping the best sleep he'd had in two years. The next morning, he moved his office from the spare bedroom to the basement, and drove to get his new and improved family at the hospital.

He introduced Hailey to her new home, and gently laid her down for her nap, in the crib he'd put together the weekend before.

Then he headed downstairs and got back to work.

Chapter Eight
Of Washing Machine Buzzers
and Poker

Three more months of phone calls, untold gallons of McDonald's coffee, and endless bank and angel investor meetings. The answer was never fully "no," but there weren't any substantial "Yes" answers either, yes being defined by a check. Wayne's patience was reaching its end. He made that abundantly clear at a board meeting in early March, a week before his call to Pope and Talbot.

While I hadn't had a lot of confidence in the green fields mill idea, I felt that buying an already exiting mill and converting it would greatly increase the odds for success. He just had to find the money to do so. I jumped in with both feet now, both as an investor and a board member. I knew this young man was not going to quit, and I was going to do everything in my power to help him. The other two men at the table that night, Jack Morrison and Bill Hart, felt the same way. We believed in Wayne and his idea. Still, after two years of fundraising and paying skeleton salaries and legal fees and incorporation costs and environmental impact studies…

It was beginning to sound like an old song. Once again, Wayne had about $100 grand left to work with, and that was it. He wasn't getting to first base on that.

"Wayne," Bill Hart began, "I've been thinking about this, and I believe you've left one stone un-turned."

"I'd love to hear it," Wayne answered.

"Seller financing."

There was a pause as Wayne processed this. "You mean—?"

"I mean, have Pope and Talbot carry your loan."

"Why would they do that, Bill?" Wayne asked.

"Why wouldn't they?" Bill answered. "They've got a mothballed mill in Wisconsin on their books, and no buyer but you. What do they have to lose?"

"Okay, but we still have to finance the de-inking plant and the change-over. This is a good start, if they go for it, but how do we do that?"

There was another long pause. It fell to me to break it. "Wayne, what Bill is suggesting is to re-start the Ladysmith Mill, and produce tissue, as they've always done. We think you should put the de-inking plan on hold."

Wayne is a pretty stoic guy, but I could see this was a bit tough to hear, and why wouldn't it be? For two and a half years, he'd been working all day every day on Plan A: de-inking waste paper, converting it to pulp, and selling it to the paper companies. He'd studied this process, lived and breathed it since he was at Waldorf. He left the company to launch this vision. He rewrote his business plan and investor memos a hundred times, pitched the plan a thousand times, had raised $340K from friends, family, and investors on this vision. Now, his Board has just suggested he toss Plan A aside and make a hard left turn toward buying an existing paper mill and producing tissue as it had for a hundred years.

"Don't answer now," Jack Morrison interjected gently. Unlike Bill and myself, Jack did not come from the paper business, but was a mentor and a strong personal supporter of Wayne's. "You need to think about this."

"Yeah, Jack. I do."

Jim Collins, in his bestselling book, *Good to Great, Why Some Companies Make the Leap and Others Don't*, makes a compelling argument for "getting the right people on your bus." Essentially, it boils down to this. A great company is not great because of its product, no matter how groundbreaking or zillion-selling it may be. A great company is made up of great *people*, focused and united on a single mission. The mission might be important in attracting those great people, but the world and its markets change on a dime out there. Great people will remain great, on *any* mission. And part of what makes them great is the ability to adapt, adjust, or change that mission when conditions demand.

Yes, Wayne had focused all his energies on Plan A. He believed in this mission, and had bet nearly three years of his life on it. Still, he was never going to get there without a miracle. It was a Hail Mary Pass, offering to buy the Ladysmith Mill for no money and have the seller carry him. Frankly, I was skeptical. I didn't think he had a prayer of a "Yes" answer.

However, it was obvious to his Board, and was becoming obvious to him that this was the only chance he had. If that mill were to sell to someone else, it was game over for Wayne Gullstad and CityForest.

It really came down to what Wayne told me in our first meeting. Was he gambling everything, just to recycle paper into pulp and be successful at this venture, or was he truly committed to creating value—for employees, shareholders and customers? Something that would last after he was gone?

Either answer was fine, but as far as Ladysmith, Pope and Talbot and CityForest were concerned, it was time to choose.

Three days later the phone in Wayne's office rang. He grabbed it on the third ring. Odd, it was after seven p.m. "CityForest, Wayne Gullstad speaking."

"Mr. Gullstad, please hold for Bob Vanderselt."

There was a moment of mild panic - well, maybe it wasn't so mild. Wayne had left word for Mr. Vanderselt, President of Pope and

Talbot's Consumer Products Group. He was pretty much the #2 man at the company, right under Peter Pope himself. Wayne didn't expect a callback until tomorrow, it was after seven, after all.

Of course, he'd forgotten about the two-hour time difference in Portland. It was only just after five there.

Wayne's panic was over the now-spinning dryer. The corporate nerve center of CityForest had been sharing the basement with the Gullstad family laundry for more than three months now. Wayne always made a point of making sure the washer and dryer weren't running when he was on important business calls. A buzzing dryer doesn't quite convey the image he was trying to maintain as CEO of CityForest, especially not to the President of the Consumer Products Division of the company to which he was about to make a substantial offer.

He'd started this load of socks, pajamas, and onesies forty minutes ago. It was going to buzz any time now. He was on a hard-wired desk phone, with not nearly enough cord to reach the dryer, and—click! Here came Mr. Vanderselt on the line.

"Hello, Mr. Vanderselt, thanks for the quick callback." *Gulp.*

"Of course, Wayne. And call me 'Bob'. How's it going back there?"

"Oh, just about right. Say, let me get straight to the—"

"And how's that new baby?"

"Oh, she's great. The reason I was calling—"

"My secretary put your thank-you note and her picture on the bulletin board," Mr. Vanderselt kept right on going. Wayne was literally breaking into a sweat, watching the dryer's timer. "She's a real cutie, Wayne."

"Thank you, sir. And thanks again for the diapers. "

"It's our pleasure. Now what can I do for you?"

"I'd like to set up a meeting, Bob. We're ready to make a firm offer on Ladysmith."

"Well, that's terrific." Bob Vanderselt sounded genuinely pleased, and perhaps a bit surprised. "That's great news, Wayne."

"We've been in meetings here at the office all week," Wayne continued from the laundry room, "and I believe we've got a solid direction to make this happen finally."

BUZZZZZZZ!!!

"So I'd like to head to Portland asap, Bob," Wayne blurted quickly, hoping he'd covered the dryer alarm.

There was a slight pause before Bob responded. "The whole team's coming to Minneapolis next week, Wayne. Let's put it on the books."

"Great, Bob. Thanks."

"Oh, and Wayne?"

"Yes, Bob?"

"Your cookies are done." Vanderselt was chuckling as he hung up the phone in Portland.

On Tuesday, March 16, just before nine, Wayne entered the conference room at the Minneapolis Hilton with Frank Vargas. Across the table from him was the team from Pope and Talbot: Mal Belafronto and Bob Vanderselt from the Consumer Products Division, Gary Hayden, General Manager of P&T's Eau Claire mill, and Ron Gasper, Corporate Controller.

"So Wayne, I'm curious," began Bob Vanderselt, as the greeting portion ended and they settled down to business. "What other operations does CityForest have going right now?"

Even with the dryer buzzer in their phone conversation fresh in his memory, Wayne held his best poker face. "Bob, the de-inking plant is our only focus right now."

Whether Wayne had decided to abandon Plan A at this point, I don't know, and he won't say. It didn't matter to these guys and it didn't matter now. He had his game-face on to negotiate the sale of this mill, and he wasn't leaving without that "Yes."

You could have heard a pin drop when he verbally spoke the offer that was in the document in front of them.

"Four million, seller financed at eight percent. First two years interest-free, with no amortization. Third year, interest only."

The men from Pope and Talbot were career businessmen, masters themselves at the boardroom poker face, but they were not remotely prepared for this offer. Either Wayne Gullstad was joking or he was nuts. There was a long silence. Remembering one of Fred Gullstad's negotiating lessons to his boy, Wayne held fast to the oldest rule in the book - he who speaks first, loses.

Finally, the CFO spoke. "Were you considering a... down payment, Mr. Gullstad?"

"No, Ron, we'll need a hundred percent financing."

I can only imagine how pleased Wayne's dad and his business school professor would have been at the obvious "stones" required of the young entrepreneur to make an offer like this - buying this mill using their money. A lot of years, a lot of shoe leather, and a lot of No's had brought Wayne Gullstad to this moment; a guy who, two years ago, couldn't bear asking bankers and professional investors, much less friends to invest in CityForest, did not even blink at the hard and incredulous stares from these executives at this outrageous offer.

And it really was outrageous. But like all good poker players, Wayne could only play the cards he had, and he had to play them well. He knew that a dark mill was not only a bleeding and depreciating-by-the-day asset for Pope and Talbot (and one they had to get off their books), it was also a black mark in the eyes of the community they had left behind. The P&T management were good guys. They had wanted a smooth and seamless transition with a new owner, but it hadn't happened.

Wayne also knew they weren't about to restart the Ladysmith Mill. That was the only real and logical recourse left to them with no buyer, but that is a capital and labor-intensive undertaking. They were better off letting Wayne do it for them. And if he failed - my opinion is, they thought he *would* fail, by the way - P&T would just take it right back, and pick up where they left off, fully operating again.

Unlike that first big deal he proposed to the Chinese Consul five years before, Wayne never once asked himself why Pope & Talbot was taking him seriously. It didn't matter. Wayne Gullstad was the one with the idea, and the gumption and confidence to ask for what he wanted, and he was all they had. Most importantly, he knew it.

There were some half-hearted attempts at negotiating, but the P&T guys knew exactly where they stood. Wayne wasn't moving from his initial offer.

Nine hours later, he got his "Yes."

Chapter Nine
Team

Cathy Bates hesitated before answering. "Could you repeat the question, please?" she asked the interviewer, sure she'd been asked a trick question. It was August 1993, and the former Pope and Talbot employee had come to the Ladysmith Mill to apply to CityForest now, for the same job she'd held for twenty years. She looked around the room. The five other "candidate-team-members" watched and listened carefully.

"If no-one from electrical is immediately reachable," the Interviewer repeated his question, "and there's no team leader present, which course do you choose, A or B? Would you like me to repeat A and B as well?"

"No, I got it. My answer is B. I shut the machine down."

"Repeating, It's not your primary job, you're not sure if the danger is serious, and restarting could take half the shift. You still choose B?"

"If I feel there's a danger, I don't wait for it to get worse. I shut it down. Period."

Cathy Bates was an experienced winder, a veteran who knew her way around the mill as well or better than anyone in this room. By the way, her answer was correct.

What Cathy had expected to be a predictable one to two hour process of filling out an application for the new owners and sitting through a quick interview had actually turned out to be a fairly intensive, all-day team assessment. Groups of candidates, some who'd worked here before the Pope and Talbot closure, and some she'd never seen were tested on their basic verbal, math, and job skills. Then the real fun began:

Each candidate was placed in a group of six, and given a puzzle-based problem to solve, both individually and as part of a team. Once a basic proficiency was determined, the candidate's assessment was laser-beam focused on the latter: *teamwork*.

The process was facilitated by two men from an outside consulting service: Gary Denny and Jay Dishnow, who quickly trained Wayne Gullstad and his new Vice-President, John Panning, in their method. Cathy remembers Wayne only as very polite, quiet, and unassuming that day. Didn't talk much, just listened. If they hadn't told her, she would have never guessed he was the CEO.

Lunch was good, too.

There were two follow-up interviews, and Cathy was re-hired. The Ladysmith Mill was a week from restarting.

I don't want to gloss over the closing of the Pope & Talbot Mill. Especially in this new economic era of plant closings and layoffs, it is a poignant and powerful backdrop to the story of CityForest. For one year, that mill was dark.

Ladysmith, Wisconsin is a small town, the Rusk County Seat. Rusk County has the lowest per capita income in the entire state. The paper mill is the second largest employer in this town - nearly a hundred of Ladysmith's 4000 people work there. Probably another hundred own or work for businesses directly impacted by the mill. Its closure was a very big deal, and the aftershocks reverberated long and loud. A lot of people moved away, some sat idle for a year with no work available, and a business or two already on the edge anyway decided to throw in the towel.

The psychological effect on a mill town closing its mill is profound, and not in the least positive. I don't want to overstate it, but this is how small towns can start to die.

The people in Ladysmith might have been a bit wary or even suspicious of this stranger who'd just bought their mill, but once they saw that he was dead serious about starting it back up, their own self-interest very logically took over, along with a newfound sense of hope and optimism. Not only was the start-date rapidly approaching, it looked like things were going to be done a little differently out there at the mill.

Nearest and dearest to the CityForest CEO's approach to management was the Team concept. Probably due to a combination of his athletic experience and studying the management style of the most successful Japanese companies, Wayne had long before adopted the same philosophy as Jim Collins, in the famous author's corollary to the "right people on the bus" concept:

"If you really need to 'manage' someone, you've made a hiring mistake."

Put simply, Wayne didn't want to make any hiring mistakes, if indeed they could be avoided. He engaged the services of Workplace Transitions, a management consulting group, in creating a thorough assessment of each candidate by assembling key staff already in place, both in the office and on the floor, getting to know the candidate as a person, far better than the standard job interview would allow, and then making the hiring decision a Team Decision. Wayne's genuine passion for empowering his people was probably the deciding factor in my coming on board at CityForest, both as a board member and an investor. It was a passion I had developed in my own management career.

I know from experience, there is no surer way to break the spirit and creative instinct in a person than give them a repetitive, one-task-only job, and look over their shoulder constantly to make sure they are performing that job *your way*. I learned while running a couple paper mills and a sawmill that not only does your productivity skyrocket when a worker has creative and operational control of his area of responsibility (and the freedom to perform any task in that area of responsibility), you have a far happier workplace and a better management-labor relationship. You also usually learn there may be a better way than *your way*. The only way to find out is to give your people the power to think for themselves.

"I imagine we all have had a work experience or two where we say to ourselves, 'If it was me running this place...,'" Wayne reflects on this approach now. "Suddenly it dawned on me as we issued the press release and started hiring staff - *I do run this place*. Now I have the chance, no, the <u>obligation</u>, to put my ideas into action. I wanted CityForest to run on what's known as a High Performance Team Concept."

In a nutshell, Wayne's interpretation of the High Performance Team concept boils down to the following 5 points:

1. Minimal layers of supervision and management
2. Real Decision-Making Authority at all levels
3. Recognition of individual initiative and tolerance of mistakes
4. Open Book Financial Disclosure to the entire company
5. Respect, Respect, Respect... to all.

The result of this Team Approach, for any company? A multi-skilled group of employees, one of several teams who can move about laterally between jobs, being rewarded for their productivity, not simply for the hours they occupy on the premises.

Some of you may know from your own experience that this Team Approach to not only hiring, but performing, multiple job tasks is not necessarily compatible with a traditional union work structure. The consulting group Wayne brought in actually specializes in this very "transition," from an authoritarian structure to a high-performance team system, which is exactly what Wayne was doing. Pope & Talbot had been a traditional union shop. CityForest would not be.

This was more a practical, than an ideological approach. Restarting this mill was going to be a lean and mean process, and if a union labor force with clear and stated limitations on job descriptions and expectations of each employee were mandatory, there's no way Wayne could have actually pulled this off. Too big, too expensive, too much infrastructure. It probably would have scared off at least some of his eventual investors, and the mill might never have restarted.

The union/non-union debate is a long and distinguished one, and not the subject of this book. It does bear mentioning in one simple thought, summed up best by the old saying, "If management would just do right by labor, you wouldn't need a union."

It was Wayne's intention to do right by the people at CityForest. He input a profit-sharing plan for the employees. The Team concept was aimed at expanding and improving each worker's job skills and increasing his or her pay accordingly. It also included open and regular communication of the company's financial health. From management's point of view, open communication here is a double-edged sword.

Honesty and transparency are the best ways to build any team, but in the first couple years at CityForest, there wasn't much good news being communicated. Some of it was downright scary, and could have scared off some very talented people. But each time there was a crisis, Wayne's honesty and openness had the desired effect. The people could see the facts and judge for themselves what was going on in their company and in their industry.

Wayne Gullstad was not some corporate "fat cat" manipulating the labor force to make obscene profits for himself on their backs. He was one man - honest and open, who'd obviously gambled everything to give this mill, and to some extent this town, a second chance. Hard times, and there were plenty of those to come, would only create a firmer resolve in these folks.

Most importantly, though, the bedrock management philosophy at CityForest was one of a deep and abiding respect for each of its employees. As my coauthor Howie Klausner describes the Clint Eastwood Approach: tell the worker what is needed, and get out of his way so he can deliver it.

An employee who is part of a well-trained team, independently empowered to make his or her best judgment in doing the job most effectively, is far more productive than one who is individually micro-managed and works under the cloud of fear of making a mistake. Judging by the fact it was the **employees** who turned away union representatives when they came to discuss organizing, it would seem Wayne and his Team Approach did indeed do right by them.

The mill had been "mothballed" carefully, and this helped the restart process immensely. This is a tribute to both the integrity and the optimism of the workers the year before. It would have been easy, and perhaps understandable in the disappointment of losing one's livelihood, for the operators, machinists, and millwrights to simply pack up their tools and go home, but they didn't do it that way.

They carefully prepared the plant and the machinery for a long, hard, and dormant winter; covering machines, draining fluids, cleaning the place top to bottom. Pope & Talbot kept a couple guys on payroll to run the boilers periodically, left the power on for heat, and hired a security company to keep the place safe and quiet. When a year passed and the new owner had taken ownership, the Ladysmith Mill would be ready to rock.

Now, the initial plan in acquiring the Ladysmith property was to make use of its physical assets and experienced work force to build the de-inking pulp mill. This was still Plan A, as Wayne walked out of the Minneapolis Hilton with his deal with Pope & Talbot, but converting that plant from a tissue manufacturer to a recycling facility was still going to be a very expensive enterprise. Even if Wayne's continued fundraising for CityForest was a roaring success in the weeks immediately following (and it wasn't), there was virtually no way he could have that facility up and running in six months' time. Fortunately, Plan B was not only in place, it was actually part of the purchase arrangement proposed by the sellers, and it made perfect sense.

Pope & Talbot was still very much in the tissue business, and they still needed product. When Wayne signed the purchase agreement for the Ladysmith Mill, he also signed a contract to produce and deliver 800 tons of tissue per month to them, at the market price.

Now it was a matter of hiring back the workers, starting up the machinery that had weathered a very cold winter just fine, and cranking out the product they were set up to crank out, to a waiting customer.

Plan A would have to wait 'til CityForest got its sea legs. They had a customer and a contract, and they were going to deliver.

Well, even if it was the deal of a lifetime - buying a fully operational mill for no money down and no debt servicing for a while - the need for capital was greater now than ever. The $4.5 million deferred and seller-financed was a great start, but that's all it was—a start. CityForest would need at least $1 million to throw the switch, and there was less than 10% of that in the company checking account as summer began. True, Wayne had attracted more than $300,000 in two rounds of private equity investment, but he'd put a pretty good dent in these Development Phase funds, covering everything from accounting and legal to environmental. He was still months away from drawing a paycheck himself, while twelve feet deep in the work of running a company. The daily realities of owning a large industrial property were descending on his Day-Planner, and the financial reality was again front and center.

Wayne needed to raise more capital, and he needed help. He turned to Bruce Davis, Deputy Director of Wisconsin's Northwest Regional Planning Commission.

Bruce acted as agent with the State, the county, the city, and the power company servicing the mill to provide the necessary start-up capital of up to $1.6 million. It wasn't without its difficulty or drama.

The Wisconsin Department of Development committed to $750,000 tied to the number of jobs CityForest created (again) in Ladysmith. When delays and a market down cycle hit the company hard its first year, the D.O.D. pulled out, after only funding about half of their pledge. This wasn't a small matter. Wayne made his opinion of their reversal well understood at a meeting in Madison. This could very well mean the very jobs they were interested in creating would never come to be, but they were un-moved.

As was he. He thanked them for their initial investment, even if they were going back on their word, wrote it off to the standard CYA mentality of bureaucracy, and kept moving forward. The clock was ticking.

In all, Wayne would raise $1.25 million with Bruce Davis, and that was sufficient to re-staff and restart the Ladysmith Mill.

At seven o'clock on a warm and sunny September morning in 1993, the first shift of the Ladysmith Mill threw the Tissue-Making switch. After three very difficult and often discouraging years of trying, Wayne Gullstad had reached the first peak of what he'd set out to do.

CityForest was open for business.

Chapter Ten
When it Rains, it Pours

It started out like gangbusters. CityForest had hired a top-notch group of Team Members, most of whom were veterans of the paper-making industry, many from this very facility. They needed little or no training in the production of tissue, which was the Best Case Scenario for a rookie CEO filling out his management offices and implementing his High Performance Team concept. Wayne's first hire was John Panning, vice president in charge of Finance. Next up, Mike Feiler came to head up Sales and Marketing. Finally, industry veteran Cliff Bienart was named Vice President in charge of Operations. Cliff was an engineer, trained at the South Dakota School of Mines, with a solid background in tissue manufacture. It was a good team.

Restarting the giant #1 and #4 paper machines went smoother than anyone could have expected, even with the proper shutdown and storage. As though there had been no downtime at all, the Ladysmith Mill was quickly pumping out the giant 102 and 148-inch rolls of single and multi-ply tissue at the rate of 40 tons a day. In their third month of operation, CityForest was actually turning a profit that in virtually any new venture is unheard-of.

And then, as 1993 came to an end, the wheels started to come off.

In November, Pope & Talbot, CityForest's primary customer, suddenly began rejecting deliveries. Thirty percent of the tissue City-

Forest was producing for them was failing P&T's Quality Control. To gain a little perspective on that, any reject rate over <u>five percent</u> is considered a serious problem. But *six times that?*

Wayne and Cliff Bienart were baffled. They were producing the same quality tissue from the same mill, supplying the same company who'd owned and produced it the same way before. If that weren't bad enough, Pope and Talbot reduced their order at the end of the year, citing a softening of their market.

Then one November afternoon, a forklift hit a light fixture, showering sparks on some freshly dried, brand new tissue rolls below. The paper of course burst into flames. In seconds, a half-ton was destroyed. That was nothing compared to the damage done by the automatic fire suppression, which was triggered immediately. Water blasted from the sprinkler system exactly as designed. There was no significant damage to the mill, but 300 more tons of tissue were wrecked. That's what insurance is for. The loss wasn't devastating, but it was unnerving.

Meanwhile, as it cyclically does in the paper business, the world markets began fluctuating. The cost of the scrap paper CityForest purchased to make its tissue jumped from $200 per ton to $260, which all but erased their profit margin when you factor in the quality control problems, which had yet to be even diagnosed, much less resolved. The market was indeed softening, CityForest had signed contracts with other customers besides Pope and Talbot, and already they were cutting shipments. Their first profitable months were a distant memory when the July '94 numbers came back significantly negative.

These both pale in comparison to an incident in June, which was truly devastating indeed. A multi-ton stack of raw materials toppled over in the warehouse, literally crushing a female employee. She survived a few days before finally succumbing to severe internal injuries. She was 47.

Perspective comes into hard, crystal clear focus in the aftermath of a serious accident, especially one with a fatality. Like most heavy industries, despite every possible precaution taken, the manufacture of paper is a dangerous business. Occasionally, awfully, people die on the job. There was no negligence. OSHA investigated the incident and cleared CityForest of any wrongdoing.

But that didn't bring her back.

The impact of something like this on a small town cannot be overstated, or even fully understood unless one experiences it first-hand, and Wayne experienced it first-hand. There was never any blaming done by anyone, accidents happen. The town came together and wept at the memorial service, patted each other - and Wayne - on the back, and in due course, put it behind them. There was nothing else to be done.

The young CEO did all the right things under the circumstances, but it wasn't without pain and a fair amount of inner guilt. The questions he began to ask himself went far beyond the scope of a Master's Degree program or any sort of executive training. *What if I hadn't bought this mill? What if I hadn't had this Big Idea to begin with?*

The answer was painfully obvious. Wayne felt this loss personally. He knew this woman. It didn't matter whether it was rational or not. He felt at least partially responsible. A woman working at his plant had lost her life.

And so began the most difficult time in Wayne Gullstad's 36 years.

The business went from struggling to *really* struggling. The quality control issues with Pope & Talbot had crescendoed into a full investigation by Wayne. He simply refused to accept the fact that 30% of the tissue leaving his Mill with a clean bill of health was rejected as defective on delivery. It was passing their own very rigorous quality check, which was implemented by Pope & Talbot to begin with. Still, the problem persisted for weeks. Finally, exasperated, Wayne dispatched an employee with a degree in statistics to P&T to walk him through their analysis methods. It didn't take him long to figure out that Pope and Talbot was making an error in its own calculations, misapplying the data in the system they had created.

There was nothing wrong with the tissue at all. They were just doing bad math!

It was a victory, but it was a small victory. They had wasted weeks of valuable time chasing down a problem that didn't exist. Meanwhile genuine problems were growing into monsters.

Though CityForest's own investigation largely exonerated the company and their quality control issues, their own due diligence and that of an outside consultant delivered a sobering verdict on their production of paper: CityForest was ranking in the 95th percentile in tissue production operating costs. Let me put that another way, so it is crystal clear: 95% of competing mills could produce a ton of tissue for a lower cost than CityForest. That's not just a slightly embarrassing statistic; it is a harbinger of doom.

Simply put, they were losing money at the current rate of production. Any sustained appreciable change upwards in the cost of raw materials would spell the end of CityForest. Almost on cue, when this bad news data came back at the end of August, the cost of scrap paper skyrocketed from $260 per ton to over $500.

And then... it started to rain.

The National Weather Service had predicted severe showers the second week in September, but even they were surprised by the Days of Noah that arrived with a vengeance in Wisconsin. It rained, and rained, and rained. Then it rained some more.

These weren't showers—these were downpours. Sheets of water that would not stop. Logs, trees, and debris floated down the Flambeau River when the water level went over the top of the dam. Wayne watched a half-sunk boat still attached to its trailer tumble past the mill. On September 15, the river breached the walls of the far side of the dam. A new torrent barreled furiously toward them, as the water level around CityForest began to rise.

And rise some more.

The mill was shut down, but a bunch of employees had made their way into work anyway. They were loading sandbags as fast as their hands and backs would allow. Any equipment that wasn't nailed down was moved to higher ground, the rest covered and protected as best they could. Despite Herculean efforts and the 100-year-old masonry walls that withstood untold tons of water pressure without breaching or even cracking, four feet of water filled the basement. Things like giant electric motors and coils, which couldn't be moved. lived in that basement. The damage was unavoidable, and it was substantial.

If all this weren't difficult enough, an internal executive matter the next month pitted both John and Mike against Wayne in a stock ownership issue. As CityForest foundered, and they seemed no nearer to converting to a de-inking plan - the reason they'd signed on to this company in the first place - the executives wanted a larger share of the company. Wayne asked them to hold off this discussion until he could make sense of the storm they'd just sailed through, and settle on a solid direction. They refused, and quit.

We've all had tough years, but I might nominate this one for a spot in the Entrepreneur's All-Time Top Ten.

1994 began with the heady optimism of three straight profitable months for the new company that had re-invigorated this small town by re-starting its mill with a revolutionary new Team Management style. It ended in the painful aftermath of a fire, a tragic accidental death, a sharp downturn in the paper market alongside a sharp upturn in operating costs, a dismal production record, a terrible flood, and the less than happy departure of two of Wayne's four-man executive team.

As Wayne sat in the quiet of his office in an empty mill at New Year's, thinking back on and staring at the year's rough numbers (a loss of $290,000), there wasn't much about 1994 to get too terribly nostalgic about. He could be forgiven for quoting the old saying, "Careful what you wish for; you just might get it."

But he didn't.

In the midst of this parade of muck, a single diamond of a memory stood shining, front and center.

One of John Panning's last duties before departing was assembling all the appropriate operations and cost data from the flood for CityForest's insurance claim. For literally a week, half the employees had been there - many 'round the clock - protecting, then cleaning and doing repairs at the mill, readying it for an amazingly fast restart.

But the Time Cards were missing. Hours worked were not appearing on the shift logs, though John and Wayne both knew these people were present, doing the back-breaking work of saving this plant from a 200-year flood - 12 and 15 hours a day! Something was going on here.

It didn't take long to figure out the discrepancy.

Except for a nominal sign-in, the employees had just not turned in most of their hours worked during that time. And it wasn't an oversight. It was deliberate. One of the millwrights spoke for them all with his explanation:

"We just didn't think the company could afford it."

It goes right back to the core values Wayne had sketched out and committed himself to back in business school, as he was dreaming of and planning the company he would someday run: **Honesty, Integrity, and Accountability**. These weren't values he demanded of his employees; they were values he demanded of himself. The people he hired showed him they had these values already.

They weren't hourly employees filling sandbags and carrying heavy equipment out of harm's way for some extra overtime dollars or a trade for future vacation days. They weren't ordered onsite. They came on their own. Some of them had to paddle a canoe to even get there.

These people were on his Team. They knew the truth, top to bottom, because it had been communicated to them. They knew this man from out of town wasn't going to run away at the first sign of trouble. They knew their company was struggling, and they knew why. And they weren't going to let it die, if they had to carry the #4 machine out to dry ground on their very backs.

The CityForest Team was family.

This is who the people of Ladysmith are. Now that he'd been with them over a year by this time, Wayne was not surprised by any of this. It was enough to plan out and look forward to 1995, comforting himself that these were the people he served, and that next year couldn't possibly get any worse.

Chapter Eleven
The Fight of His Life

It got worse.

Wayne arrived at the February 1995 Board meeting, bruised and battered from the previous year, but still optimistic. The numbers weren't complete, but the preliminary forecast he'd gotten from his new Financial Controller showed a modest loss of only about $40,000 for the month of January. This wasn't bad. All of us had expected it to be more than twice that.

However, when the Controller arrived and delivered her report, the numbers actually revealed a loss of $265,000. It was a showstopper, to say the least. It was incomprehensible to Wayne that they could have lost so much. There must have been some sort of software glitch or data problem. It was unsettling, but these mistakes do happen.

Then it happened again. The next month the forecast was again for a modest loss, but the actual figure turned out to be nearly $300,000 on sales of $950,000.

Besides the obvious problem of a financial controller who was actually a very capable executive but not a very talented accountant, there were clearly some serious obstacles that had to be addressed immediately. A company cannot bleed like that for very long, and survive, especially one with limited cash reserves. Something had to be done, and it had to be done fast.

"One of my favorite professors at UCLA told us again and again that there are only three ways for a company to make more money," Wayne tells me. "Raise prices, cut costs, or make your people work harder."

"Well, we were working as hard as we could, we really couldn't raise our prices and keep the customers we had. We had to figure out a way to change our cost structure."

The answer was tough to arrive at, and took an outside company to help them find it at all, but it came down to something very simple: CityForest would need to modify its prep system so they could buy cheaper grades of scrap paper. It was a relatively simple operational change, but like we all know, the hardest thing to change is people's minds, especially when an idea flies in the face of *the way we've always done it before.*

There was sound reasoning for the wide skepticism among the troops in making top of the line tissue paper with cheaper materials. There was a vigorous debate throughout the company as Wayne put it before his Team. The majority were against this operational change. Many of the old-timers dug in and flat out declared, "It won't work."

This wasn't exactly a showdown, but it was going to be a critical moment in this company's history.

It's time to return to our 12 Steps. Up to this point, Wayne had been riding the ups and (mostly) downs of his young company. This was the first true test of his leadership.

10. I Make Decisions.

In his bestselling book, *The Travelers Gift*, author Andy Andrews reminds us that the purpose of analysis is to come to a conclusion. This seems logical and obvious, but it's not always so easy, especially when there is a chorus of people more experienced than you pro-claiming for all to hear that your conclusion "won't work."

Wayne and Cliff Bienart had plunged themselves into an analysis of this quandary. The "simple solution" of changing their stock prep process might work. Then again, the old-timers might be right—it might not work. Regardless, there was a significant cost involved, significant effort, and significant pushback from his production team.

The words were never said, but it was always there; this rookie CEO was just that—*a rookie.* Wayne is a calm and relaxed individual with a cool head on his shoulders, but he'll never convince me that there wasn't just a whiff of self-doubt when a thirty-year veteran paper converter looked him in the eye and told him this idea of his was a waste of time and money.

As Harry Truman so famously said, although not originating the phrase, "The buck stops here." Ultimately, a leader, a CEO, even the President of the United States is paid to do just one thing: make decisions.

Wayne had no choice but to try. If it didn't work, it didn't work. But doing nothing was clearly not working either, and would surely lead to this company's early exit from the tissue-making scene. He didn't pass the buck. He made his decision and, following the 11th Step, he **acted on that decision.** Swiftly.

"Courage?" Wayne laughs incredulously when we recall these days. "Courage is jumping over a fence that might have a big dog on the other side, but it's not courage if there's a <u>bigger</u> dog chasing you on <u>this</u> side. It's your only option."

There was a very big dog chasing CityForest as the first quarter came to an end. They wouldn't survive a year of this bloodletting. They had to jump that fence.

"Wayne, I strenuously object to this idea." Cliff Bienart had been arguing with Wayne for over an hour. The new system was in place, it was working, and the CEO was ratcheting it up even further.

"Cliff, we have no choice."

"We've reduced the cost 120 bucks per ton! I mean, that's incredible! It worked!"

"I know, Cliff. but it's not enough. We're still bleeding cash, bad."

"This is a mistake, Wayne. This will pit one production team against another, and that will get out of hand."

"If we collapse, what will it matter?"

By the end of March, the new production method using lower grade fiber had indeed reduced their costs by nearly $120 per ton. Wayne was sharing the daily cost-saving results company-wide, including the fact that some teams were reducing costs more than others. He decided to propose a friendly competition between teams, and Cliff was adamantly opposed. He feared it might backfire.

Again, there just wasn't time to debate it, and it worked.

Cliff's concerns were justified, but the entire company knew just how dire their situation was. This was about their survival. Every day, each shift came roaring online like they were hitting the field for a championship game. In one month, they shaved another $50 off each ton produced. That knocked their operating cost down nearly $150,000 per month!

Oh how I would love to tell you that this was the Turnaround. It wasn't. Sadly, it was too little too late. CityForest still lost $185,000 in March and another $170,000 in April. Things were improving, but these were egregious losses. Cash was critically low, the company went late on some purchase orders just to make payroll. Some of the creditors and suppliers put us on a cash-only basis. At the rate we were going, we'd be out of money by the fourth quarter. With the trend of these numbers, CityForest wasn't exactly a prime candidate for further investment or even a loan extension.

It was time for something even more radical.

Wayne was exhausted. I could hear it in his voice in our daily phone calls, and definitely see it in his eyes when I was on-site; This young man with a young family and 85 employees in a company on life support was dealing with a crisis daily, and rapidly moving toward burnout. He doesn't remember not sleeping, but I remember a weary and worried CEO that spring. I knew he was burning the midnight oil searching for an answer, something new he could try, anything he might have missed.

It was a struggle for the young family as well. Wayne had kept his salary low, Carol had continued working, but financial and time pressures were increasing by the day. I could hear in his voice, even with his eternal optimism, the toll this was taking on them both. Carol had miscarried twice. It might have happened anyway, but the stress of this continuing drama couldn't have helped.

I was on the board of this company, and I was an investor. The corporate by-laws say my fellow board members and I had a fiduciary responsibility to do whatever was necessary to guide and advise CityForest. But my "fiduciary responsibility" was not on my mind as we contemplated our next steps. It was something light-years beyond that.

When we hear and talk about business in this country, the emphasis is always on the success of the venture, and certainly on money. What usually gets little more than a footnote or an after-thought is, in my view, actually what this whole thing is about.

Since I took that first phone call from Wayne Gullstad out of the blue, advising him and making a financial investment in his Big Idea, the purely business side of my stake in this company had taken a back seat to something far more lasting and important: I had truly come to care for this young man. For all the reasons that I have chosen to write this book, I began to look on him as I do my own sons and daughter.

Mutual admiration aside, we had some knock down-drag out arguments in those twelve difficult months, especially the week I came to the mill and went over every inch of the operation, top to bottom, making a study of things we might do to save this sinking ship. I made no secret of my opinion that Wayne just didn't have the experience to handle a situation so critical and so complex. Needless to say, he didn't exactly see eye to eye with me on that. In exasperation, and not exactly brimming with affection, Wayne abruptly walked out of a meeting with, "You remind me of my dad, Web!"

I've been in business a long time, and I can recognize a kindred spirit. I didn't just believe in the big vision of CityForest, Wayne's cutting-edge management philosophy, or even his very obvious intelligence and ability. I believed in Wayne Gullstad as a person. He wasn't tying himself in knots because the market was beating him, or even that his company was losing money. He's a competitor. He wasn't happy about either, to be sure, but I knew the root of his worry was for the people who had put their trust in him; his investors, his employees, the town of Ladysmith.... and his young family. That is a heavy load to carry when things are going south.

My concern was for the company, of course, but my bigger concern was for this young man and the burden he had chosen to take on. I was a Board Member and his friend, and I wasn't about to let either one fall through the cracks.

At the Board meeting on June 1, Jack Morrison, Bill Hart, and I went over the financials and my findings from the week spent in Ladysmith. I had recommended that CityForest bring on an experienced manager to come alongside Wayne and Cliff Bienart, and steer them through this crisis. Jack and Bill did not agree. They believed the only course left was for me to step in and temporarily take the helm.

"Oh man," I remember saying to myself. "This won't go well."

And it didn't. When Wayne arrived for the meeting, the idea was put before him, and his response was predictable. I imagine it felt like being kicked while down. The "discussion" was intense, and it went into the night.

Honestly, I didn't think it would work, either. I'm not exactly a soft touch and I believe I've more than chronicled Wayne's Norwegian stubbornness. I envisioned an endless uphill battle, and feared that for the rest of his life, Wayne would consider calling me in 1991 as the worst mistake he had ever made.

But Bill and Jack were not to be moved. In their eyes, it was this course or shut the mill down. After nine hours, I think some combination of Wayne's exhaustion, Bill Hart's ticking off the critical financials and insistent recounting of my experience as a paper industry CEO, and Jack Morrison's gentle mentorship and guidance turned the tide.

Wayne agreed to step down as CEO of CityForest. He would stay on as president, but I would be given day-to-day executive control of the company. He would later explain that reaching this decision came down to one thing: there just weren't any rabbits left to pull out of the CityForest hat.

"Sometimes, heads do have to roll," Wayne says with an ironic chuckle now. "That's a tough call to make anytime, but it's *really tough* when one of the heads is your own."

I left Minneapolis the next morning for Portland to gather some clothes and personals, buy a new laptop, then turn around and head back to Ladysmith, Wisconsin before the end of the month.

I didn't get much packed. My phone rang June 20, and it was Wayne.

"I can't do it, Web. I'm not stepping down. Furthermore, I want you to resign from the board."

If Wayne's nights had been sleepless leading up to the board confrontation, the three weeks following were probably something close to torture. The initial sense of relief he felt was followed by the deepest remorse he'd ever known, and, I'm sure, anger and at least a little betrayal. Carol had initially said nothing when he informed her of the Board's decision. Wayne thought she too would feel a sense of relief.

He was wrong.

Carol was truly the fifth board member of CityForest, even if she didn't carry the title. She was a stockholder, though, and had advised him all along, not only as a supportive wife and partner, but also as a now-seasoned Fortune 500 executive. She was under no illusions about the state of this company. She could read the monthly balance sheets and cash flow realities, and see a distressed market, operational struggles, and the just plain awful luck of the first year as well as any of us.

Yet, in spite of the pressures and difficulties this situation was bringing on this young family, it bears repeating that Carol's blood ran Entrepreneur Red. It was the only life she'd known as a child. The Gullstads had nearly five years of blood, sweat and tears - not to mention money - wrapped up in CityForest. Their family and friends had invested and, quite bluntly, she'd be damned if she would just stand by and watch her husband meekly hand it over to the rest of the board and me.

"You built this company, Wayne," she declared to her husband when she finally broke her silence. "You've got the right to tank it."

It was the only true fight that either of them can now remember in their twenty-year marriage, but Carol wasn't backing down. She knew her husband had never been a quitter, and she wasn't going to let him start now.

Men at war will tell you that there is a strange sense of peace, even in the direst of circumstances, once clarity has been achieved. Even if your odds are less than one in a thousand, when there is simply no option but to fight your way out, even if it's to the death, the heart and mind are more settled on their singular course. And usually, it takes a shock to get to this point.

Wayne wasn't expecting what we hit him with at that fateful Board meeting, and it was a devastating blow. Nine out of ten would have packed it in and quit in a huff, or just meekly stood down and let the Board do what it deemed best. Both scenarios were anathema to him. Carol simply spoke what was in his heart anyway.

I look back on it now, and cringe that we ever made this suggestion to begin with. CityForest **was** his company, and even with his lack of experience, he wasn't doing anything appreciably wrong in running it. He'd made his share of mistakes, but he didn't own the patent on that one. All of us had.

Still, I have to admit, I was combative when he reversed his decision and asked me to quit. "I refuse to resign" I shot right back, knowing that he couldn't fire me.

"Fine," my stubborn young friend returned the volley. "You will not be re-nominated when your term expires in December."

We hung up full of macho energy, though deep down I respected the fire that was clearly still in that belly, and I was secretly happy to hear its return. Truth told, with the benefit of time, I can say now that *I* was the one who was relieved. To this day, Wayne and I remain close. He is like one of my sons to me, and I laugh now, knowing he was true to his word: he did not re-nominate me.

My guess is he slept just fine the night he made his decision to stay.

Three very difficult months later, CityForest regained profitability. As this market goes, supply and demand swung again. The price of scrap paper collapsed, while demand for tissue went up. The improvements and innovations they'd made in their production methods were significant, and now permanent. Before the year was out, the mill had gone from **losing** 300 thousand to **making** 300 thousand per month on sales of $1.5 million.

The CEO of CityForest had fought his way out, and he had not required his Board or me in doing so. This was his fight… **his and his company's.**

"I didn't blame the Board," Wayne says now, of the incident. "They were just trying to do the right thing for CityForest, and of course for their own investment of time and money. I probably would have done the same."

Then Wayne adds a very telling observation, which takes us right back to the Twelve Steps we've been talking about all along.

"I tend to be optimistic, stubborn, and a little naïve. I just feel like I'm never beat, but I guess that's the definition of tenacity. Work hard, stay positive, and be too dumb to know when to quit."

Chapter Twelve
The Project

Remember Plan A? CityForest was actually born with a business plan to convert the Ladysmith tissue mill into a de-inking pulp mill. It would cost about $25 million, which was 15 million less than if they built it from scratch, and they had the advantage of an experienced labor force. It was a good plan - expensive, but good.

Now, aside from two very difficult years and the long uphill slog to profitability in making tissue, there were some other compelling reasons for Wayne to file Plan A permanently and make Plan B that much better. Not the least of which, while he was fighting to keep CityForest alive in 1994 and 1995, a gaggle of other outfits decided to try his Plan A out for themselves. The federal government had jumped into the act by providing huge tax-exempt financing for recycling companies, which of course encouraged the construction of these plants. This, and a very favorable lending climate in America's boom-time 90s, brought some big players like Lake Superior Fibers and Fox River Fiber into the de-inking pulp game. Even if CityForest could raise the necessary $25 million, there was virtually no way they could compete with these guys.

Plan B, making tissue like the mill always had - only better - may have been a slight disappointment to Wayne's Recycling Big Picture for CityForest, but it was a blessing in disguise. I think ultimately, it saved the company. Plan B became permanent.

Now it was time to make Plan B better.

What is it the US Marines say? That which doesn't kill me, only makes me stronger? Wayne emerged from those two years stronger... much stronger. The company was better, profitable now, their process leaner and more economical, their CEO battle-tested—and smarter. There was no way he was going to go through two years like that again, but he knew he couldn't relax. If he sat comfortably on his lead, coasting through these profitable times, he'd eventually face that monster all over again

At the November Board meeting (my last, by the way), Wayne unveiled to us The Project. It was a comprehensive set of improvements aimed at solving the mill's cost, quality, and delivery constraints. In brief, it was a complete overhaul of the Ladysmith Mill, intended to keep what happened to them in '95 from ever recurring. It was big, it was ambitious, and it was very expensive.

Wayne had asked three companies to put together proposals for a major re-build of CityForest's Paper Machine #1, and for a complete state of the art de-inking system, to supply the paper machines with the pulp needed to make the tissue. Voith-Sulzer, the German manufacturer, had a better idea and proposed building a whole new paper machine, rather than an upgrade, which could never achieve the same results as a new unit, no matter how extensive the rebuild.

I want to make sure my non-industrial, non-paper-business readers fully grasp the scope of what we're discussing. When we talk about a 'paper machine,' we're not talking about a printing press or something you might see at Kinko's. This is a giant, multi-faceted apparatus encompassing a boiler, pulp slurry processor, huge dryers, and room-sized rollers putting out 12-foot wide rolls of tissue weighing over a ton. The CityForest plant took up more than 100,000 square feet in 1995. Paper Machines 1-4 occupied a goodly portion of that.

Let me put this another way. The Project, building a new machine alongside the de-inking facility, would cost somewhere north of $50 million, including debt service. Remember: less than six months before, this business was operating at a loss of well over a hundred thousand a month and heading for bankruptcy. Now, three months into profitability, the CEO-founder is bringing a plan before his Board for $50 million of new debt?

Was this guy nuts?

No, he wasn't. This was the very sober calculation of the captain of a ship that had just weathered a storm that, for all intent and purposes, should have sunk him. To take this maritime analogy one step further, the captain realized his boat would not survive another hurricane like that. It was just too old and leaky. He couldn't control the next storm, but he could fix up his boat.

Okay, let's get back to the reality of CityForest and The Project. Wayne didn't spend his immediately profitable weeks partying at the Americ-Inn bar in Ladysmith (though I'm not sure I would have completely blamed him after the "*annus horribilus*" he'd just survived). He spent them camped out on the Ninth of our 12 Steps:

#9 I Sweat the Small Stuff

And I mean, small stuff. Wayne was a numbers guy before he started a company. He may not have loved the process of a thorough internal audit, but he knew how to do it. He studied every square inch and operation of his company with the cold objectivity of a pathologist. What he saw scared him.

The brutal fact was that the "little mill that could" remained in the bottom 5% of efficient producers in this business. The other 95% produced tissue more efficiently at a greater profit margin. When interest rates are low, and supply is high along with demand, City-Forest would sail right along, just this side of "in the black."

However, another '94-95, this boat was going down for good. They would never survive another Perfect Storm like that.

Wayne's logic was simple: no matter what they did from this day forward, they were taking a risk. The risk of launching the Project - taking on substantially more debt - was obvious. To do nothing, and go about business as usual, was risking that the market would never hit another down cycle. Nobody needed to tell this CEO that. Just like the tide, down cycles always return.

The better bet was to borrow the money and improve the company.

But that didn't make it an easy sell.

Investor and outside director Mike Pao put The Project proposal down, deep in thought. Mike was a level-headed financial mind, not given to the emotional swings of business. He was a big supporter of Wayne's, but a straight shooter and Wayne's go-to reality check. After a minute of awkward silence, Wayne finally pushed for an answer.

"So what do you think?"

"I think this is a lot of work, Wayne, and financially very, very risky."

"I've run the numbers, Mike. These improvements will put us in the thirtieth percentile."

"I see that, but you're leaving out one tiny detail. You're gonna have a heck of a time raising 50 million bucks, man. I don't think you will. And even if you do, do you really want to be on the hook for that?"

"I don't think I have any other choice, Mike."

"I can think of one. Cash out. Sell while you're still making money."

I want to stop right here. On its surface, Mike's suggestion sounds unfeeling, cold, and calculating. It's not at all.

Wayne's first objective in starting CityForest was to give a solid return on his investors' money. Mike was looking at the numbers, thought they could easily sell CityForest, a now profitable tissue mill for around $20 million. Everybody wins here: investors, bankers, Wayne and Carol, and the employees who would share in the profits. Most of the Team would probably just continue working at the Ladysmith Mill with a new owner.

Wayne is an entrepreneur at heart, and for most entrepreneurs, the game is starting, running, then selling the business. He was in the perfect position to take those profits and start another venture, and not have to climb Mt. Everest, which is essentially what taking on a debt of more than $50 million would turn out to be. This is where Mike Pao's recommendation was coming from. Why go through the pain of this? There would be absolutely no shame in taking his advice and selling the company at a 4X profit to a manufacturer that would keep right on making and selling tissue, and employing most of the same Team he'd brought in.

But Wayne had a second objective, which was just as important to him; leaving CityForest's operation with a solid future. The Ladysmith Mill was doomed to fail in the next major down cycle. It was as simple as that. Now that he knew this, there was simply no way the CEO and founder of this company was going to stand by and wait for that to happen, whether it was Wayne Gullstad at the helm or someone else.

I need to emphasize, Wayne's "Project" was not a few small repairs around the shop floor, paid for with a credit line or a small commercial loan. What Wayne was proposing absolutely dwarfed the efforts and expense of everything else he had done with this operation over two years. It was risky, it could torpedo the company with a debt it simply could not service, and it was going to be damn hard. Indeed, why wouldn't he just take the money and run?

Simple. Wayne **cared**. He cared too much about the people who'd invested in CityForest, yes, but he also cared about this business he'd given his life to these past five years, and he very much cared about the people working at his mill. He was within his rights to sell this company, take a well-deserved profit (not to mention, *rest*), and leave the future up and down cycles to the next guy. But to return to our maritime analogy, that would be like selling your boat and crew in a condition you knew would sink in the next storm.

Wayne wasn't about to do that. Though I suppose we could have voted him down, his logic, passion, and the tenacity he'd already showed convinced us not to. He was humble and sincere in seeking -and listening - to the advice and counsel of his Board, his advisors, and his Team at the mill. We all agreed with his assessment of the company, as well as the risk of disaster whichever way we went. Really, in the end, the decision was his.

And this is what leadership is all about. As we discussed in the opening chapter of this book, if you're going to lead people down what is sure to be a difficult path, first and foremost, you must care. People will not trust or follow you if you don't.

No one doubted Steve Jobs' passion when he retook the reins of Apple Corp. There wasn't a second thought in all of the US Army as to General Norman Schwartzkopf's heart in leading a half-million troops in Desert Storm. It doesn't matter whether you are talking about a major corporation, an entire army, a football team, a three-person shop in an office park, or a paper mill in Ladysmith, Wisconsin. This principle is absolute and never-changing:

To succeed long-term, you must care.

Because he did, Wayne decided to take the hard road of raising the money, overhauling the company, and risking this debt to keep CityForest alive and well, long after he was gone.

Two and a half years later, in March of 1998, Wayne was sitting in the conference room of the Chicago law firm Foley & Lardner, eyes bleary and brain mushy from "signing papers and paying attention for fourteen solid hours." Across the table were the lawyers and executives from a major bank and a large power company. He paused over the last signature, which would execute the deal to finance the CityForest Project at $57 million.

It hadn't been an easy twenty-eight months. This kind of money is tough to come by for anyone, and the quest had taken up the majority of Wayne's energies while Cliff Bienart and the Teams kept the lights on and machines running at CityForest. Happily, the company had remained profitable, as well as motivated.

In keeping with his philosophy of transparency and open communication, Wayne put The Project before the entire company. He explained it in full, both upside and risk. Along with the sobering reality that he was now placing before them, he added something further, a challenge that would make this sure-to-be difficult road worth it for every single one of them.

He named this challenge "1 IN 2000," and it immediately became the mantra and driving force of CityForest. Their new company-wide charge leapfrogged survival and simple profitability. It was now the attainment of Number One industry ranking in quality and profitability by the year 2000, which was the tissue-making equivalent of winning the Super Bowl.

It wasn't just a ploy, a CEO trying to "motivate the troops" with a tired gimmick or artificial slogan. Neither was it a general, undefined "we're number one!" kind of opening whistle cheer for each shift, and it was not a competition between production teams.

This was a measurable goal, an objective for the entire organization. Everyone from the CEO to the summer intern now understood the stakes. As employee-owners, they all assumed the risk of The Project right along with Wayne.

Wayne turned to his advisors, Todd Barocas and Sam Al-Imam, the men he had entrusted to find and structure the financing of The Project. This meeting represented a lot to them as well. They had both been about the very difficult and often maddening job of marketing this financing package: lining up investors, finance companies, and banks, presenting the deal, and structuring corporate bonds and loan agreements to scores of prospects. When this process began, both Sam and Todd were working for capital companies who ended up abandoning this sort of deal-making enterprise, but each man believed in CityForest and the viability of this venture enough to partner up as free agents, and soldier on.

It all came down to this in a Chicago conference room. After two years of searching, presenting, discussing, and running down one dead end after another, Wayne turned to the last page on the last document in a stack of documents two feet high, awaiting the final of what had seemed like a hundred of his signatures today. Across the table sat the representatives of Union Bank and a power conglomerate called ENRON.

Union Bank would enter in with a corporate loan of $27 million. ENRON, who was at the top of their game in 1998, was in for $30 million as a subordinated lender.

Wayne signed the last page, and shook hands all around the table. He stepped out in the Chicago night air for a late-night walk and a cigar. The Project was under way.

Chapter Thirteen
Deja-Vu, All Over Again

The 16-month construction phase was barely complete when a new storm hit the market in late 1999. Energy costs shot up again, as did interest rates. The cost of fiber was well on its way to doubling. The much-deeper-in-debt CityForest ship was struggling to make all the new pieces fit into its operation as the industry was headed straight into another down cycle, and this one would be even deeper than the one in '95. Still, confidence was high that once the new equipment went online, the capacity would nearly double, and the operating cost would decline. CityForest was poised to start a new era in its history.

But when the Project went online in the Fall of '99, the opposite occurred.

The problems showed themselves immediately. The changeover process in machinery like this is monstrously complex, with loads of heavy, intricate, and very expensive moving parts. Ask any mechanic of any machine and he or she will tell you: the more moving parts, the more that can go wrong. Murphy's Law - *if something can go wrong, it will* - always applies here, and it applied with a vengeance in the installation and start-up of Paper Machine #4. Voith Sulzer and CityForest personnel worked round the clock, but just couldn't make the thing produce anywhere near its capacity. Worse, they couldn't figure out *why*. Across the mill, so many systems were interlinked that solving one problem almost always created another.

Both "worst case scenarios" of production problems and an ever-softening market were coming to pass the end of 1999; The Perfect Storm for the Project.

Which is not exactly the optimum situation to be in, when servicing a debt of $57 million becomes a monthly reality. It was beginning to feel, as old Yogi Berra once put it, like *déjà-vu*, all over again.

Voith Sulzer is a German company. This particular machine's components were designed there, manufactured at its facility in Brazil, and shipped to Ladysmith where it was assembled and placed online. Murphy's Law is the rule, not the exception in a global undertaking like this. There were at least three languages flying in the design-fabrication-installation process (German, Portuguese, and English) It was inevitable there would be misfires at some point, and there were. After nearly a year, Paper Machine #4 was performing at less than half its projected rate of 88 tons per day, when it was online at all. Even after essentially tearing it down and putting it back together, something clearly was not right.

In CityForest's contract with Voith-Sulzer, there was a provision for a damages payment should the machine fail to achieve its guaranteed production level, but that didn't matter to Wayne and the rest of CityForest. They just wanted the thing to work! The success of the Project, not to mention their goal of 1 in 2000, positively depended on it. In May of 2000, it failed again.

It took an outside consultant six weeks to finally track down the problem with the giant machine. It was the 60-ton roller in the "black-magic infused" Yankee Dryer (a gigantic, game-changing machine that spun at over 6000 feet per minute). The roller's face had to be reground. It was as simple as that. Well, simple in theory, but a micron-precise bear of an engineering task. Happily, the engineering teams of the CityForest, Voith Sulzer, and a consultant company were able to pull it off. By the end of June, the machine's production leaped almost to capacity.

Sadly, though, it was looking like it might be too little, too late.

As the year 2000 wound down, the Perfect Storm in the market-place didn't abate, it only intensified. CityForest was playing catch-up in a whirlpool of rising costs, shrinking demand, and an extended price slump for tissue. This ship was now in the stormiest seas ever. In January 2001, two months before their semi-annual payment on the subordinated debt of $30 million came due, the company contacted ENRON to let them know they would not be able to make that payment.

ENRON. If there was ever a company name that summoned up a more immediate and visceral image and response, I never saw it. What in the world was CityForest doing in business with what would become the pariah of American corporate culture, and why would this giant power company lend this little paper mill in Wisconsin $30 million?

ENRON was, first and foremost, a trading company. When they rose to spectacular heights in the 90s, they began diversifying and venturing into new areas, applying the same trading skills they had used successfully in the energy markets, their specialty. What initially drove ENRON to CityForest was simple: they would sell them the necessary natural gas and electricity. Further, they were providing themselves hedge opportunities from both types of energy, as well as hedges on waste paper and finished goods like tissue. Lastly, it was simply an equity-like partnership loan. They saw a good investment in an up and coming tissue manufacturer with a great expansion plan, and they <u>made</u> that investment.

Now much has been written about ENRON in the last few years, The company's fate and fallout from their horrific crash is well-known. What's also well known and documented is their reputation for being unscrupulous and occasionally downright shady. This was not the case with the CityForest arrangement.

Two of their toughest, most seasoned negotiators, Dick Lydecker and John Enerson, were the ones sitting across the table from Wayne Gullstad in Chicago when he signed the mountain of equity and loan documents three years before, and they would be sitting with him again soon. No doubt, Wayne dreaded this meeting, but not for any reasons beyond the inability to meet his obligations to people he truly revered and respected.

"There were obviously some integrity-challenged guys inside ENRON, especially at the higher levels," Wayne tells me now, "but I never ran into one. In all our dealings with them, everyone we worked with was tough, but unfailingly honest, straightforward, and fair. It's really a shame so many great people at that company got painted as dishonest and corrupt due to the actions of a small few."

The first meetings were not hysterical, angry, or threatening. Lydecker and Enerson were not given to dramatics. Wayne had always shot completely straight with them, and vice versa. No new territory would be covered in exploring their options. They had frankly discussed every possible outcome when they first structured this deal - from cashing themselves out to foreclosure.

ENRON had no interest in the latter. The paper business was in the tank in 2001. They would have been left with essentially nothing in a liquidation, just a $30 million write-down. They were left with two viable options: get someone else to take on the debt and their position, or take the equity of CityForest and run it themselves.

At the beginning of the second quarter, CityForest reached a re-structuring agreement with senior lender Union Bank of California. ENRON agreed to take a huge loss and get out, selling their position for about 25% of its face value. However, in the wake of three new paper company bankruptcies, there were no takers. Even Union Bank, well seasoned in the paper business, passed on the opportunity. ENRON was stuck with this little paper mill in Wisconsin.

But ENRON didn't *want to be* stuck with a little paper mill in Wisconsin. This was not even remotely their core business. Their only realistic course was to take over most of CityForest's equity and run the company, and who would they logically ask to do the hands-on management? The Team that was already in place, of course.

By summer, Wayne and his Team would lose 90% of their equity in the company they'd built, but at least the mill was still open and there was a "claw-back" provision for them to pay their way back to their original ownership position. Unlikely, but it offered a glimmer of hope. There would be three or four months of negotiations between ENRON, Union Bank, and a third investment group, but the ship was now out of the storm.

It is at least slightly ironic that by that fall of 2001, the Ladysmith Mill was shattering all their previous production records. The #4 paper machine had worked its bugs out, #1 was roaring along like gangbusters, and the de-inking plant was fully online. The Project had finally hit its stride. Wayne's original vision of a recycling and de-inking facility had been realized ten years after, and his mill was producing more and better tissue than ever before, at the highest efficiency rating in its history. Even in an ongoing soft market after the September 11 terrorist attacks, they were profitable again, three months straight.

The company was saved.

And yet, the company wasn't going to be Wayne Gullstad's anymore. The young man with the independent streak, the passion, and the tolerance for high, high risk - the Profile Entrepreneur - would be that in name only now.

The sign on the gate still said CityForest in late 2001, and the management decisions were still Wayne's, but the reality was that the founder of this company would technically be working for someone else.

Chapter Fourteen
The Harder I Work, The Luckier I Get

Then, like a meteor from the sky, Wayne's reality was turned upside down by a truly cataclysmic event. On December 2, 2001, ENRON, poised to become a majority equity-holder in CityForest, declared bankruptcy.

Tens of billions of dollars literally vaporized into the black hole left by the energy trading company's spectacular fall. In days, their glass and steel behemoth of an office building in Texas was empty, and the oldest and largest accounting firm in the United States disappeared in the whirlwind. Most of both companies' senior management were immediately put under indictment. The ripple effect of ENRON's collapse is still with us.

But for CityForest, the ripple effect was profound in the other direction. The deal they had worked out with their junior lender had languished for weeks between lawyers and the Arthur Andersen Accounting offices, and had *never actually been signed*. Not only was there suddenly no controlling equity partner for CityForest to answer to, there was no one at ENRON to sign the deal. Therefore, there was no one to collect on CityForest's $30 million debt, either!

Step #8, I Will Be Lucky

Now, don't laugh too hard. There would certainly be settling up in the future, with someone, but in his wildest imaginings, Wayne

Gullstad could never have envisioned something like this. He truly grieved for the thousands of ENRON investors and retirement funds who'd lost untold amounts of money, and for the job loss and permanent stain on the employees there who did it right (which was the vast majority of them), and for CityForest, who was still in default on their debt to them.

But the fact remained, it would be months before federal regulators and the courts got around to organizing a Creditors' Committee to sort through ENRON's wildly complex bankruptcy. The CityForest loan was such a small blip on this radar; it would be nowhere near the top of their priority list.

There was suddenly, just before the holidays, no one to whom CityForest could even submit payment on their loan. Effectively, the now-profitable tissue manufacturer had been given an interest free loan; a loan with no payment for the foreseeable future.

Merry Christmas.

Maybe it is okay to laugh, certainly not at the pain and ripple effect of this company's fall, but the irony of the timing of it for Wayne and CityForest.

I suppose with the mega-dose of Principle 8-A over the previous years of perfect storms (*I will be unlucky*), CityForest was overdue for the balancing of that equation. But I have to tell you. Though I have seen lots of people get lucky in my 60 years in business; never in all that time have I seen a miracle like this. Days from signing away the equity of all that he'd worked so hard to build for ten years, just to keep his company from complete ruin, Wayne Gullstad gets a reprieve like something out of a Frank Capra movie.

Let me be clear. There would be a settling up. The debt wouldn't just disappear into the ether. Wayne is an honorable and responsible man, who fulfills his obligations.

But he's not an idiot. For the moment, there was no one to whom this obligation was due. What this "reprieve" really meant to CityForest was TIME. It was a chance for the ship to right itself while ENRON's bankruptcy process went forward. Wayne knew that ENRON's creditors would come calling eventually, but it would be a while. In the meantime, CityForest had a chance to build a head of steam, service their debt to Union Bank, while actually building up some capital reserves and continue upgrading all levels of the operation.

Their luck continued. The market was beginning to turn, as the shock of September 11 faded. Fiber and energy prices were dropping. Several of CityForest's competitors had fallen by the wayside in the last down cycle. This was that second chance we all pray for now and again.

CityForest didn't look the gift horse in the mouth. Wayne and Cliff stepped on the gas, and the company kicked it in to Overdrive.

It took a year and a half for the ENRON Creditors' Committee to approve a verbal settlement agreement with CityForest, and it was a favorable one. John Enerson, exonerated of any wrongdoing, had remained at the now-bankrupt company to help manage its liquidation. This was also a blessing, as John was well familiar with their operation.

Though CityForest had offered up a restructuring plan, the Creditors' Committee had no interest in an ongoing ownership of CityForest, nor were they seeking any possible future equity position. They wanted cash… now. There could not have been a better negotiating position for Wayne. With the help of his advisor Mike Knight, CityForest proposed a steeply discounted cash price to ENRON to take out the debt. It worked out to be about 20% of what they owed.

And oh, to be in a negotiation with an unemotional party wanting to conclude terms as quickly as possible, and only interested in whatever cash they could get. ENRON and the Creditors' Committee agreed to the terms. $30 million in debt would be retired for about $6 million.

Wayne made sure to get that one signed on the spot.

The storm was now really over. The glimmer of light on the dark ocean CityForest had been sailing burst into a bright sunrise. Financing $6 million was a breeze compared to what they'd been through before. Why wouldn't it be? They were a company with a completely upgraded operation who suddenly had $24 million less in debt than they had the year before. They raised much of it in cash through their shareholders and the State of Wisconsin's Investment Board, and rolled the rest into a restructured agreement with Union Bank of California, their senior lender, with an annual payment that was $3 million less than before.

In 2004, as if on cue, the Overdrive Phase CityForest had entered as The Project went fully online and paid its dividends. Fiber costs were still dropping, and the company's operation had increased its profit margin by over $100/ton. That yielded a net profit of $5 million on $43 million in sales in 2005.

Were they lucky? Oh lord yes, no two ways about it. But did your dad used to say the say the same thing mine always did?

The harder I work, the luckier I get…?

The question isn't will I get lucky? You will. In case you skipped all of Book Two up to this point, Wayne is living proof that the Entrepreneur, like all people, will be *un*-lucky, too. It is as certain as Murphy's Law.

The question Step #8 demands you answer is this: what will you **do** with your good and bad luck? It reminds me of the other thing my dad used to hammer into my head:

It's not what happens to you, it's what you DO with what happens to you.

Put this one in the bank. Memorize it and repeat it every day. Because this, more than anything else, will determine whether you fail or succeed as an entrepreneur or anything else, for that matter. What do you do with your good luck? What do you do with the opposite? That's what makes or breaks you in business and life in general.

Wayne and CityForest lived Step 8-A over and over again. They didn't deserve their run of bad luck any more than anyone else does. "Stuff"... happens. Truth told, as bad as '94-95 went, he could be forgiven for quitting. Many, if not most, would have handed the keys over to me and the Board, and run screaming into the night.

But he didn't. He just worked harder. Even that didn't work in the short run. The heat got hotter, and his company was looking the Grim Reaper right in the eye. Wayne remains a relaxed, still fairly stoic guy with an always positive outlook, but he will never convince me that he didn't have a few late nights alone in the office, asking himself, "what have I gotten myself into?"

Then came a once in a million years lightning bolt break, but that's not what turned CityForest around. It's what they did with that break.

And what about the company challenge? 1 in 2000?

No, they didn't make it by the target date. It took seven more years for the complete vision of Wayne Gullstad to become a reality. In 2007, they attained their goal. CityForest became the industry leader in tissue manufacture, a cutting edge recycling and de-inking facility, and a healthy profit-making investment for its shareholders.

More importantly, they had built a company that would be quite healthy when its CEO and founder decided to pack it in and move on... and that day was approaching rapidly.

Chapter Fifteen
Family

It all came down to Family.

When Wayne Gullstad incorporated CityForest in 1991, he was a 33 year-old newlywed with a wife working as a Fortune 500 executive. Fifteen years later, the battle-tested CEO was a father of four, commuting back and forth between Seattle and Ladysmith, Wisconsin. Carol was a full-time Mom now, and Dad hated leaving home more every time he left the house for SEATAC airport. The major goals of the entrepreneur had been realized. CityForest was at full stride, growing stronger by the day. Lee Luft, the new company president, not only ran the operation flawlessly when Wayne was in Seattle, he did the same when Wayne was on-site, as well.

The Gullstads moved back to the West Coast in 2001 to be near Wayne's mother who was getting up in years. Seattle may have been a hefty distance from Carol's folks, who were still in Southern California, but it was sure closer than Ladysmith, Wisconsin. It wasn't an easy or convenient commute for five years, but central to Wayne and Carol from Day One was the idea of family. Wayne knew that every day he spent away from his children he was missing some new milestone or magic moment. And what was the point of having kids if you were never around?

Still, there was no CityForest exit plan, before a chance conversation Wayne had in Green Bay in 2006.

The man was a customer of CityForest, and a kindred entre-preneurial spirit for Wayne, that enthusiastic "always-on" idea guy. Wayne loved traveling over to call on him. He always had some new idea to combine their two operations and partner up. He was in the restaurant and travel paper business. They converted tissue and other materials into everything from napkins to maps and toilet seat covers, and his company was very successful.

Expecting just their usual shop talk, status of orders, and maybe some new "next big thing" idea over lunch, the guy floored Wayne with a full-blown proposition to merge their operations in creating a new company, taking the new entity public in two or three years. It was a solid plan. If the 15 years as CEO had taught Wayne anything, it was the ability to spot fatal flaws in any plan, and this one didn't seem to have any. As a matter of fact, it made sense. Flying home to Seattle that weekend, he could think of nothing else.

It was raining in Seattle, not that that is news. Two of the four kids squealed with delight, and filed the house with war-whoops as they rappelled down the "secret compartment" Wayne had added in his home remodel a couple years back. Carol studied her husband's face as he stared out the picture window from the kitchen table. "So what are you thinking about anyway?"

"How much I love just being here at home." He picked up a new team picture of his daughter Hailey with her middle school basket-ball team. "How much I hate missing their ball games and plays."

"You don't miss that many," Carol reassured Wayne, pouring each a fresh cup of coffee.

"I honestly never even thought about it 'til now, Carol. Leaving, I mean."

"You could always step down as CEO and remain on the Board."

Wayne smiled. "Pity my successor, having the founder of the company watching his every move from the Board." He shook his head. "Naah. If I'm gonna break from it, it has to be all the way, for everybody's sake."

"Well, Wayne, I'm not gonna tell you we wouldn't rather have you home seven days a week. We're doing just fine, but it's not the same when you're gone."

"We're on the same page here."

"Okay, then. Let's look at the timing, and look at this possibility from CityForest's point of view," Carol answered, sounding as focused and direct as she surely did as a vice president at General Mills.

This is what he loved about his wife. She could easily separate the two issues, business and personal, and analyze this the way she would a company. Carol had been a *de facto* partner in CityForest every step of the way, even as a stay-at-home Mom. He never made a significant decision without having a conversation just like this one with her.

"The shareholders are making money, the company's making its best profits ever, and the community likes us." Wayne answered.

"How critical are you to any of those?"

Wayne nearly spit out his coffee, laughing. He was way too modest to ever assume any credit for the company's successes, and humble enough to own the blame for the failures. "I'm serious, Wayne. This is your deciding factor."

He sipped again, thought, then drew a happy and satisfied sigh.

"It's the Team, not me. I am very replaceable."

Now I realize if we take a sampling of the weekly business magazines, this would be perceived as a personal liability, not an asset. After all, global business meltdown aside, this remains the era of the Rock Star CEO, the bigger than Life Entrepreneur. Celebrity status for the guy or woman at the top of the company seems to be a sort of Media Holy Grail these days. That's all well and good for that indi-

vidual, and it's usually well and good for that individual's company...
until that individual is gone.

Business history is littered with companies who were founded
and/or run by these larger than life personalities. I have no doubts
you can conjure three or four right off the top of your head. But what
happens to the companies we immediately associate with this "rock
star" type persona, when that rock star departs, or sadly, dies? Nine
times out of ten, that company founders, many times it dies itself,
and takes a lot of good people with it.

Wayne's philosophy in running CityForest took the exact opposite approach, by design. He certainly never attained rock star status,
which from the stoic Norwegian's point of view was fine by him.
More importantly, though, Wayne had from Day One surrounded
himself with a team of talented professionals and engineers. He was
under no illusion that the Ladysmith Mill needed him on a day-to-
day basis.

If this merger and IPO came to be, CityForest would probably
have a nice party for him, there would be many laughs and surely a
few tears. And the next day, they'd be right back at it, without missing a beat.

Yes, not only could Wayne bring himself to forming an exit strategy, now was actually an excellent time to do it.

Only, it didn't come to be. Not this time, anyway. The devil is
always in the details in these things, and once both companies really
drilled down into the nature of a partnership or an outright sale of
one to the other, it didn't really make sense for either of them. They
agreed to go back to their original customer-vendor relationship, no
harm no foul.

But his two-month exploratory experience in 2006 wasn't a
waste of time and energy at all. It revealed to Wayne and Carol that,
in fact, after all these years of living, breathing, and thinking City-
Forest 24/7, they were ready to let the company go.

After a long talk with his management team and the Board, Wayne sought out a good broker to market CityForest. He found the perfect match in the Minneapolis Investment Banking firm of Greene Holcomb & Fisher. They had all the right attributes for a sale like this—experienced and well-connected in the industry, personable, smart and honest. Happily for them, CityForest was at the top of their game right now. Record production levels, and still could barely keep up with their orders. More profitable than ever, with continued upward projections, and the market remained storm-free: low energy and raw materials costs, high demand. And, oh yeah, one last little detail. They'd finally hit their goal of being number one in the industry in quality and productivity.

There are essentially two types of investors that would consider buying a company like CityForest: financial and strategic. The financial buyer may know little or nothing about the business he is buying. He is doing much as he would when buying a stock - for the return on investment. The strategic buyer, however, has a vested interest in the particular business that company is in. They may already be in that business. They may even be a competitor.

One or two financial investors kicked the tires on CityForest, but predictably moved on once they got a good look at the size, scope, and complexity of the tissue-making operation. Too much work for them. Besides, they took one look at the numbers and were immediately skeptical. The company's trend upward from 2000 seemed too good to be true.

The strategic buyers weren't skeptical. They caught on quickly and, in a very short period, Cellu Tissue Holdings of Alpharetta Georgia emerged as the lead prospect. The negotiations were smooth, friendly, and fairly fast.

In true American Dream fashion, the Entrepreneur went out on top. On March 4, 2007, Wayne Gullstad signed the closing papers on the sale of CityForest.

Due to a confidentiality agreement, Wayne was not able to disclose to me at our celebratory dinner the price he got for the company. Still, having been there at the beginning and still friends after a very rough mid-point, resulting in my "retirement" from his Board, I had to press.

"Well, Web, let me put it to you this way. You remember those first investment rounds, when we sold in blocks of $20,000? At closing, each of those investments returned over $500,000 after taxes, and the employees split nearly $4 million from the Share Plan we set up."

"So you consider this experience a net gain?" I asked, doing the best I could to keep a straight face.

"Yes," the stoic Norwegian smiled slightly. "CityForest was a net gain."

For a lot of people, I might add.

A Final Thought
Three Entrepreneurs and a Wannabe

There has been more than a small dose of irony in the writing of this book.

This project began simply enough, in my desire to tell the amazing but true Horatio Alger type stories of three positive thinking, hard-working guys and their attainment of the American Dream. That was it. I was proud of these guys, proud that I could be a part of their success. I just wanted to put it down for the record.

But like most ventures, including the ones chronicled in this book, the road we end up riding is rarely the road we initially set out on. Two things turned Plan A into Plan B: the economic meltdown of 2008 and a good long look in the mirror.

I told you at the beginning of this book that I am rich. It's true, in spite of the fact that my personal net worth is decidedly less than when I started this book, since the Perfect Storm that hit Wall Street like a tsunami last year, I have been very fortunate in these eighty years. The one thing that was missing was the fact that I never closed my own loop as a businessman by making a go of it as an entrepreneur. I did have my own business selling magazines as a child during the Great Depression, but from that point on, I was always working for someone else. Again, there's not a thing in the world wrong with that. I just always dreamed of starting a venture of my own, and seeing it come to life.

Until I began this book with my coauthor, I thought I had satisfied that longing by advising and guiding Anthony-Ross and CityForest, calling on the experience and knowledge gained in my near half-century in the business world. But as my coauthor, Howie Klausner, kept peppering me with the same question over and over—*what are we really trying to say here, Web?*—the answer suddenly became obvious, and a bit unsettling.

The message and lessons this old CEO-storyteller wants to leave his reader with are a lot broader than just two interesting and exciting company histories. I wanted to try and wrap them in the fundamental truths of this life that seem to get lost in all the noise and hype of the business literature, media headlines and talk shows, and even business academia that surrounds us. It's more than overwhelming, it's contradictory, and it's confusing. Quite honestly, if I were just graduating and preparing to start a business today, I don't think I'd have a clue where to even begin.

When we hammered out the 12 Principles, which became the 12 Steps, Howie and I both realized that our message was much broader in scope than two inspiring "you can do it!" stories. There were lessons that needed to be taught or, more modestly put, reminded. Advice we all need to hear, and hear again and again.

That's when it got unsettling.

Who was I to give out advice? To teach principles? To speak with any authority beyond a lot of years living and working? Like I said at the beginning, if you were looking for the thoughts and observations of a Rock Star CEO or a Washington policy wonk or the head of a business school, you bought the wrong book, and I apologize.

But it was *this very thing* that my co-author and I agreed on. Those folks have spoken aplenty. How about a different point of view, from one whose credentials are only those years and these experiences, and the lessons he's learned?

My life went full circle when Howie Klausner and I shook hands and decided to do this. Just like Tom and Rob, and Wayne and his wife Carol, your two authors were deciding "to go for it," assume the risk, of time and money to produce this book, and work tirelessly in getting this message out there, especially at this critical moment in American History.

There are no guarantees here. As we prepare to go to press, we are not aligned with a major publisher. We have no distribution deal in place. The preparation for this book represents several years of my life, and the actual writing, nearly a year itself. My coauthor, and now partner and I both feel very wonderfully successful in having created this book, but just like the men profiled in these stories, we can definitely fail in the marketplace.

And yet, like Tom Ross, Rob Anthony, Wayne Gullstad, and the millions of others who have stepped out on that ledge and opened their venture up for business, the measure of our success isn't so much the market success of our product. It is in the people we serve, the lives we live, and who we become in the meantime.

The humorous irony of this book you are holding is that you and I, dear reader, have just changed places. It is you now, who witnesses the beginning of Mr. Klausner's and my start-up. And ultimately, determine not only our success in the marketplace, but the degree to which we serve.

In the meantime, I am happy to note that after eighty years, I have closed the loop. Like my son Tom, and Rob Anthony and Wayne Gullstad, and the millions of others who have made this country the nation of which I remain so very proud, I have opened the doors of *The Entrepreneur's* Way.

I am finally... *truly...* an Entrepreneur.

Epilogue

On Rescuing
the American Dream

Greatness is never a given. It must be earned. Our journey has never been one of shortcuts or settling for less. It has not been the path for the faint-hearted — for those who prefer leisure over work, or seek only the pleasures of riches and fame. *Rather, it has been the risk-takers, the doers, the makers of things* — some celebrated but more often men and women obscure in their labor, who have carried us up the long, rugged path towards prosperity and freedom...

Starting today, we must pick ourselves up, dust ourselves off, and begin again the work of remaking America. Our challenges may be new. The instruments with which we meet them may be new. But those values upon which our success depends- *hard work and honesty, courage and fair play, tolerance and curiosity, loyalty and patriotism-* these things are old. These things are true. They have been the quiet force of progress throughout our history. What is demanded then is a return to these truths.... a new era of responsibility — a recognition on the part of every American that we have duties to ourselves, our nation and the world; duties we do not grudgingly accept but rather seize gladly, firm in the knowledge that there is nothing so satisfying to the spirit, so defining of our character, than giving our all to a difficult task. (*emphasis, authors'*)

President Barack Obama
Inaugural Address, January 20, 2009

I cannot leave this book without visiting this moment in our American History and asking the President of the United States a very pointed question:

Mister President, do you mean it?

I join the people in this country in truly wanting you to succeed by using these three values you have cited to lead us out of the abyss in which we find ourselves right now: Honesty, Integrity, and Tenacity.

The writing of *Rescuing the American Dream* was really instigated by the beginning of the Meltdown of the American Economy in September of 2008. As my coauthor tells us in his preface to this book, that was the signal to him that this project was not only viable, it had to happen. I couldn't agree more.

In the last six months, we have stood by, watching shell-shocked as the American banking system has collapsed, and the major pillars of our economic infrastructure have fallen like dominos in their wake. It has triggered the worst recession the United States has ever known. The stock market has fallen farther faster than at any time in its history. 40,000 people lost their jobs in one day in the hugest round of job cuts we've ever seen. Bankers and auto company executives line up next to state governors for bailout money like it's the soup and bread I saw doled out as a child in the Great Depression. It was bad when Howie Klausner and I began in October. It has gotten critically worse in the six months following.

We could dissect the causes and factors all day long, but the root cause of all these current and very real economic woes comes down to one simple thing: People have lost faith in The System and the system won't work without that faith.

If I were to sum up the Twelve Steps of Character the Entrepreneur's Way not only exemplifies, but positively *demands*—it really comes down to two; **Honesty and Integrity**.

Above all, it is these two foundations that both Anthony-Ross and CityForest were built on. It is these two that the United States also was built on, not only in its institutions as a country, but in its very laws and most certainly, its economy.

We are a capitalist nation. Every good and true thing that has been America is a direct result of the freedom that our founding documents have given us, to pursue life, liberty, and happiness in the way we see fit, within the basic laws of society. Capitalism not only does not guarantee success, it doesn't protect one from failure, either. It is the ultimate democracy and meritocracy. It is the essence of human freedom, and it is the foundation of what we cherish as The American Dream.

But at its core, capitalism is built on trust. Without honesty and integrity, there is no trust. And where there is no trust, capitalism will not, indeed, *cannot* work.

The United States was born as a result of a lack of freedom. People came here not only to practice their religion without government interference, but also to escape the oppressive taxation and government intrusion into the freedom of how they would get along in this world financially. In point of fact, it's more than a catchy phrase to say that in 1776, we were a nation of Entrepreneurs. We really were!

It worked. Capitalism works. If we just tick down the list - from the blacksmith, the printer, and the village baker in the colonies, to the railroad, airplane, telephone, computer, television, movies, and a thousand other entrepreneurial enterprises that made this country a literal Promised Land for so many for so long - well, the fact that the US has an immigration problem makes perfect sense. Who wouldn't want to come here with that kind of freedom, opportunity, and track record?

But now, in the howling winds of this Perfect Financial Storm in which we find ourselves as we write these words in 2009, the very things that made America that Shining City on the Hill are in dire peril. There is an unmistakable attempt to essentially reverse every fundamental operating principle the United States of America was founded on. The course we have begun in response to this crisis represents a dramatic reduction in our individual liberties, our self-reliance, and the potential value and rewards of our intellect, our experience, our hard work, and our passions in the application of each of the 12 Steps of the Way of the Entrepreneur.

In its heart and soul, The Entrepreneur's Way is nothing more than the relentless, tenacious, and honest pursuit of life, liberty, and that pursuit of happiness. It is this operating code and philosophy that made this country into that Shining City on the Hill.

But this Way hangs in the balance in 2009.

This is not a Republican or a Democrat issue. This is an American Issue. We will always find something to disagree on in the American Conversation. But like a family that squabbles and argues regularly, when push comes to shove, we're still family, and where we agree is far and above where we do not.

The Answer to our current and very real Crisis lies not in one elected individual, or a program, or the government at all. Our greatness, and the answer to this crisis of faith and trust, lies in the same place it always has every single time this country has faced hardship and danger. The Answer lies in the people. That's been our secret all along.

Our government and its institutions were designed to be "of the people, by the people and for the people." When we trust those people, the whole thing works. When we don't, it doesn't.

The Anthony-Ross Company and CityForest are true and inspiring stories of the American Dream, but they are not unique. All around us, throughout the history of our land, we've seen them repeated again and again and again. As you consider your own venture, or start that venture, or examine it mid-stream, or even strive to understand and help solve the current crisis in this country, ask yourself a simple question:

Is my business, my family, my life, and even my country in harmony with the 12 Steps of Character, the 12 statements of principle that work every single time they are applied, to any enterprise, relationship, or endeavor?

Or is it not?

If your answer is yes, I hope you receive this closing challenge in the spirit in which it is given: It's time for All Hands on Deck. It is with Character, and Character alone, that we will right this ship and rescue the still-strong heart and soul of what has always held this nation together, in good times and bad... The American Dream.

G. Web Ross
Howard Klausner

Acknowledgements

I would first like to thank my wife Ella Lee, who put up with my long hours at the computer where I was non-communicative and sometimes unresponsive to her and the household needs. Of course, thanks to the Three Entrepreneurs who started this whole thing to begin with: Tom Ross, Rob Anthony, and Wayne Gullstad who spent hours filling in the blanks from my memory of their stories.

Thanks to the multitude of people who graciously gave their time for interviews. A special thanks to Dr. Nancy Wilgenbusch, past president of Marylhurst University, Ron Grover with Business Week. Holly Hutchins, retired executive with Shell Oil, Dr. Wallace Roettger, President of Lyon College, and Greg Cushman, former editor of the Bend Bulletin, all of whom provided constructive criticism of the original manuscript, which helped us greatly in the fine-tuning of the final manuscript.

More thanks to Brent Williams, President of Williams Media Group, a committed lifelong entrepreneur himself, who designed the cover, but has contributed so much more, just by sharing his creative ideas and undying enthusiasm.

And finally, last but certainly not least, thanks to my partner and now friend, Howard Klausner, who took my story and transformed it into an interesting, exciting, and informative book.

G. Web Ross

Of course, I second the authors' hearty and humble thanks to each person listed above, and would like to add a few of my own.

Robert Smith, who mentored, encouraged, and otherwise convinced me I could actually do this. Andy Andrews, whose work continues to inspire and amaze me. Dr. Charles "Chuck" Denham, whose two-day crash course of his company's operating principles and his teachings in the country's best business schools gave us the "killer-app" for connecting these two great stories. Brent Williams, everything Web said above, squared. Clint Eastwood, for letting me watch him make a movie start to finish, and whose management style is the textbook example of running a successful venture, regardless of the industry. The late great Derek Niblo who, with only the example of a life very well lived, prepared me to write a book about character and entrepreneurship, and his daughter, my wife Heather who, like Web's better half, has demonstrated the pinnacle of patience, kindness, and encouragement since the day this project began.

And finally, to my co-author Web Ross, for the great stories, the wisdom, encouragement, and the occasional friendly creative battle as he raised the bar, *again and again!* My respect for your passion and your deep belief in the goodness of people and the greatness of our land goes with you forever, as does my eternal gratitude for bringing to me the most deeply satisfying work of my career.

Howie Klausner